Victorian Feminism 1850–1900

Victorian Feminism 1850–1900

Philippa Levine

The Florida State University Press
Tallahassee

First published in Great Britain by Hutchinson Education, an imprint of
Century Hutchinson Ltd and currently published by Unwin Hyman Ltd.
Printed in Great Britain. Please address editorial inquiries to 303 Dodd
Hall, The Florida State University Press, Tallahassee, FL 32306.

University Presses of Florida is the central agency for scholarly publishing
in the State of Florida's university system, producing books selected for
publication by the faculty editorial committees of Florida's nine public
universities: Florida A&M University (Tallahassee), Florida Atlantic
University (Boca Raton), Florida International University (Miami), The
Florida State University (Tallahassee), University of Central Florida
(Orlando), University of Florida (Gainesville), University of North
Florida (Jacksonville), University of South Florida (Tampa), University
of West Florida (Pensacola).
Orders for books published by all member presses should be addressed to
University Presses of Florida, 15 NW 15th Street, Gainesville, Florida
32603.

British Library Cataloguing in Publication Data

Levine, Philippa
  Victorian feminism 1850-1900
  1. Women — Great Britain — Social
  conditions 2. Women — Great Britain
  — History — 19th century
  I. Title
  305.4'2'0941   HQ1593

ISBN 0 09 173181 X

Set in 10/12pt Times by
Input Typesetting Ltd, London SW19 8DR

Printed and bound in Great Britain by
Richard Clay Ltd, Bungay, Suffolk

. . . still we have looked, and tried, and
found that the present rules for
women will not hold us.

Geraldine Jewsbury to
Jane Carlyle, 1849

Contents

Acknowledgements

There are many people and some institutions without whose help and encouragement I could not have completed this project. The women's movement has nurtured my commitment to women's history and has sustained me in innumerable other ways. I owe an enormous debt of gratitude to the Flinders University of South Australia whose generosity extended far beyond the granting of a research fellowship.

I should like to thank the Mistress and Fellows of Girton College Cambridge for permission to quote from the manuscript Family Chronicle of Emily Davies, Royal Holloway and Bedford New College for permission to cite the Elizabeth Reid Papers and the Leisure Services Committee, Manchester City Council for permission to quote from the M/50 papers in their feminist archive. The Fawcett Library delivered up its usual mass of treasures; David Doughan's constant care and enthusiasm are always a joy. I should like to thank David too for his critical reading of sections of the book.

Margaret Cameron was also good enough to read some of the manuscript and I am grateful for her astute comments. Discussions with Janet Howarth and Jim Hammerton stimulated – and at times re-activated – my interest while Helen Jones, Beryl Madoc Jones, Liz Stanley, Gillian Sutherland and Alec Tyrrell all shared findings and opinions with me generously. Sally Fraser provided a beautiful typescript out of an ugly series of drafts in what must have been record-breaking time. I am indebted to her. My editor at Hutchinson, Claire L'Enfant, has retained a commitment to the project throughout and given me invaluable encouragement.

Friends in both hemispheres have shown a constant interest in the progress of the project. I thank them, and more especially Steve who has submitted patiently to my obsession with this work.

Philippa Levine
Australia
January 1987

1   Introduction

This study is partly an exercise in resurrection and partly a long overdue corrective to the many inaccuracies and assumptions which have dogged the history of pre-suffragette feminism. A good deal of the work on nineteenth-century feminism has concentrated on its negative characteristics, and in particular its narrow class base and its attachment to liberal politics. On closer examination, much of the thinking about the feminism of this period which has discredited or dismissed it for such reasons has been as much myth as reality. In this work, I have sought out the connections between individual feminist campaigns through their shared understanding of their own position as women and their shared commitment to a wider vision of the future.

In the first place we need to exercise some caution so that we do not simply use historical figures in order to make sense of our contemporary preoccupations and thus render them passive objects. In the context of women's protests about their own position, we need, therefore, to consider the possible range of meaning that words such as feminism might take on in specific historical contexts. After all, in a society which did not embrace even a semblance of democracy and where welfare provision was limited, for the most part, to philanthropy or the workhouse, we must understand the effect of a different set of values, the challenging of which required tactics and philosophies far removed from our late twentieth-century solutions.

Nineteenth-century England was a world in which ethical values stemmed directly from the teachings of the church. The position of women, and the construction of masculinity and femininity, owed as much to religious values as to biological difference or to the changing requirements of the economy. Women were bound doubly by its teachings; in the biblical texts of St Paul, their submission to men had become an item of religious law, and further, in the religious revivalism of the early nineteenth century, their task as bearers of religious moral values was clarified and strengthened. They were granted a role in spiritual life which at one and the same time empowered and confined them. They were empowered in that moral education became their prescribed duty in the family context, but confined in that they were thus restricted to the family responsibility it entailed.

The effect of this assumption of moral guardianship was a major factor in the creation of what Catherine Hall has dubbed the 'domestic ideology' characteristic of nineteenth-century England.[1]* In earlier periods, though women had been associated with household duties, they had shared a role in the family economy which had often taken them beyond the provision of purely domestic services. Domestic ideology, or the ideology of the separate spheres, was to idealize a situation created by the new industrial capitalism of the nineteenth century. One of the characteristics of an increasing reliance on technology in production was the marked separation of home and workplace, both because industry gradually replaced agriculture as the dominant employer of labour, and because industrial machinery was less and less suitable for use (or indeed affordable!) within the private home. In such a context, the distinction between home and work became far clearer than it had formerly been.

In practical terms, that distinction raised new problems, particularly for women. An unattended home might also imply unattended children; child-minding became a problem. The working day (or night) became more formally structured and the physical fact of going to and coming from work added time to the hours a woman worked. When, then, were her domestic duties to be fitted in? Shopping, cooking, washing were in any case doubtless nightmare tasks in the insanitary and overcrowded slums of Victorian England; how much more arduous would they be if they had to be slotted into a rigorous industrial timetable?

The ideology of the separate spheres developed at this time as a fusion of values and assumptions culled severally from religion, economic need, biology and tradition. We know, of course, and will see in the following chapters, that the ideal division between domestic woman and public man was never realized in many homes, and never became the dominant reality. As an ideology,

---

* Superior figures refer to the Notes and references sections following each chapter.

however, it was highly effective in ordering people's values according to its precepts. It is rare to find a thorough consonance between ideology and practice in any instance, and perhaps the true power of ideology might be understood for our purposes as a psychological one. If it was effective in dismissing unmarried and working women alike as society's failures, if it was effective in polarizing the traits of masculinity and femininity in the popular imagination, then surely its effects were palpable.

Ideology in such an interpretation is thus the means, the process by which existing power relations are made to appear as not simply the best possible but also the *natural* social formation. As Penny Boumelha has argued, it represents 'as obvious and natural what is partial, factitious and ineluctably social.'[2] We must, then, understand the division of masculine public and feminine private not necessarily in terms of consensus or reality but as a social construction, as a means of justifying the relative positions and organization of men and women in society as the best possible arrangement.

In practice, of course, many men as well as women felt such an ideology to be burdensome, and yet the very pervasiveness of such thinking made it difficult for either sex to find effective challenges. For many women committed to the fight for women's rights, the most effective weapon was not the total rejection of that ideology but rather a manipulation of its fundamental values. After all, if women's purity made them the natural custodians of religious teachings and values, then their effect in public life could only be uplifting. The sentiment of moral superiority became the leading edge of many women's rights campaigns in this period, not only in the more obvious area of sexuality but in more overtly parliamentary concerns as well. This championship of womanliness, though defined within the limitations of separate sphere ideology, none the less functioned as a means of making their campaigns not simply a negative struggle against unjust disabilities but a positive proclamation of their identity as women. The nineteenth-century women's movement was discovering a pride in its female identity, and its campaigns were concerned as much with promoting that optimistic self-image as with a simple call for equality with men.

This difference between men and women, instead of being a reason against their enfranchisement, seems to me the strongest possible reason in favour of it; we want the home and domestic side of things to count for more in politics and in the administration of public affairs than they do at present.[3]

This embracing of the domestic ideology was a complex and sometimes contradictory move. The centrality of the family in women's lives made it perhaps inevitable and certainly cogent as a political practice. And yet, at the same time, their calls for a domestication of the public arena, which were frequently highly critical of its values, did foreshadow a collapse of the distinction between the two spheres of public and private. Women's demands for a space in public life without sacrificing motherhood, for instance, represents an implicit challenge to separate sphere ideology even where they vigorously upheld it.

This thoroughgoing if not always obvious rejection of existing social relations, coupled with a strength and pride in their shared femaleness, set women's campaigns apart from the other reform issues prominent in this period. A host of writers have argued that the demands of women for equality within the legislature is no more than one feature of the general reforming activities so prevalent in this period. The distinctive features of women's campaigns and the singular fact that many of the individual issues shared the same body of activists does, however, suggest a qualitative distinction between the limited aims of what we call pressure-group politics and the more 'global' overview offered in this period by feminism.

The definition of feminism in the historical context is, of course, fraught with difficulties. We must be wary of determining it by our contemporary evaluations and thus deny its particular context, and yet the temptation to seize upon parallels is not always easy for us to resist. None the less, women's positive identification with one another in a context of political struggle suggests that the use of the term feminism is not anachronistic. There were so very many areas of injustice which needed attention drawn to them that we see, at first glance, a women's movement splintered into a series of single-issue campaigns to fight educational or sexual or employment battles. They were not, however, entirely separate campaigns; they drew on the same core of women whose political analysis saw each individual campaign as one facet of a broader aim and purpose. As Helen Taylor remarked to Barbara Leigh Smith Bodichon early on in the history of organized feminism,

I am sure all the various movements for improving the condition of women help one another, and all ought to go on simultaneously if we are to hope to see any considerable effect produced in our time.[4]

Taylor's assessment was echoed over and over in the ensuing years not only in individual statements but, more importantly, in the common practice of the movement.

In many ways, the feminism of these women was more of a life-style than merely a form of organized political activism. The networks they created within the political sphere crossed over into both intellectual and social areas of their lives. The early Langham Place circle of feminists in the 1850s not only initiated a series of campaigning committees and the first feminist periodical of the century, but offered the use of a library and a reading room for women in London's West End. Debating societies and social clubs exclusively for women followed, providing women with a physical space of their own, an important consideration in an age when so many women lived in the houses of husbands or fathers or brothers. This political and intellectual proximity inevitably involved a social element too. Feminists in all areas of the country not only knew of but chose to mix socially with one another. Their diaries and letters tell of teas and soirées and at-homes, as well as close sustained friendships. Educationalist Emily Davies and pioneer doctor Elizabeth Garrett were lifelong friends, while doctor Sophia Jex-Blake and housing administrator Octavia Hill were so inseparable as to invoke parental disapproval.

The close and familiar nature of feminist acquaintance suggests, of course, a high degree of social homogeneity. They shared not only a recognition of their common disabilities as women but often a similar social position too. Most, though by no means all, nineteenth-century feminists were from well-assured middle-class backgrounds. The privilege of not having to scratch a living from a set of diminishing options, as working-class women were so often forced to do, secured them the opportunity to develop a wholesale feminist analysis. They were not unaware of class distinctions; in middle-class Victorian society, constant fear of the working-classes was a dominant motif. Many women had experience of philanthropic work among the poor, an area in which some found a life-long vocation. Their feminism, however, acknowledged far more the desperate needs of working-class women than any fear of them.

Towards the end of the century, working women's involvement in women's issues began to grow, specifically in areas with as direct an interest for them as employment and trade unionism. Ross Paulson's distinction of 'equality-as-opportunity' and 'equality-as-distribution-of-income' as the respective characteristics of middle-class and of working-class feminism, while schematic, does point up the crucial concern which, of necessity, dominated working-class women's lives.[5] The wearying constancy of economic uncertainty inevitably served to distance working women somewhat from feminist involvement, leaving most campaigns largely in the hands of middle-class women.

The inescapability of that class divide has led many historians to separate out two strands of feminist thought: bourgeois feminism and socialist feminism. Marilyn Boxer and Jean Quataert, working in the European context, see bourgeois feminists as concerned principally with achieving formal equality between the sexes, while their socialist counterparts saw their feminism as a subset of socialist principles.[6] The distinction is a common enough one, but it has little meaning in the nineteenth-century English context. In the first place, socialist ideas remained largely in obscurity in England throughout the nineteenth century, hindered rather than fostered by the sharp division of class so characteristic of the nation's social profile. In neither the small socialist organizations that surfaced from time to time, nor in feminist or any other radical movements, did Marxism become common currency until the twentieth century. There were critiques, and powerful ones, of capitalism in England throughout the century, but the early successes of that economic system had entrenched it more deeply perhaps than in the European nations, where other forms of social and economic organization survived longer. Feminist reasoning did see the sexual division of labour as a crucial site of women's subjugation but its criticisms remained internal to the existing system.

The socialist feminist, according to Boxer and Quataert, identified the problems of working-class women as the principal target of her activities and was thus prominent in areas such as the organization and encouragement of women's trade unions and the like, over and above the so-called bourgeois campaigns which stressed the importance of women's entry into education, the professions or the property rights of married women. In the English context, nineteenth-century union activity was spearheaded as much if not more by middle-class feminists than by working women themselves. It may be that the specific preoccupations of the women's union movement shifted when working-class women fully articulated their needs and desires, but it is insufficient to draw a dividing line simply on grounds of class. The debate around protective legislation in England (see Chapter 5) suggests a division not so much between middle-class and working-class women, as between socialist women and working women; for while socialists applauded the principle of state intervention in employment practices, many working women sided with its bourgeois opponents, if not always for the same reasons. Theirs was a practical dilemma, torn between the Scylla of a potentially health-endangering job and the Charybdis of joblessness.

Boxer and Quataert also point to the tendency among early socialist feminists to abandon feminist campaigning in favour of involvement in socialist parties. Again, in Britain, there were no large socialist parties in the nineteenth century and though the Independent Labour Party was attracting radical women members from its foundation in 1893, few wholeheartedly threw over their specific feminist commitment. Indeed, as we will see, one of the hallmarks of nineteenth-century feminism was the close-knit sense of community whereby women's personal political differences seldom intruded as a problem.

In effect, feminist politics did not operate in the same way as male or mixed political campaigning. Indeed, it would have been difficult for it to do so, as women were denied access to existing channels of political influence. When we study feminism as a political and a social movement in this period, we must be alert to the means at its disposal and to its specific handling of those means. Thus it cannot be sufficient to categorize or criticize it in terms of a politics with which it had little reciprocal communication, for that is to mould it into inapplicable stereotypes; though we should acknowledge the limitations imposed by its narrow class base in this period, to relegate its importance merely to a movement which serviced only the needs of bourgeois women is a mistaken assumption. Jane Marcus has asserted that 'the women who won the vote and eight-hour day were sisters and allies'.[7] In seeing individual campaigns organized in a largely autonomous way as fundamentally linked activities forming a wider understanding of female subjugation, we can acknowledge fully the role played in developing that consciousness by feminists of whatever class and background.

Feminists in this period both worked within the values promoted in their own society and distanced themselves from the mainstream. They worked within the system by their increasing acceptance of the significance of sexual difference, but in collapsing the central public–private separation, they rejected its categories. This duality has led to some confusion; historians have attempted to assess feminism in terms inadequate and unsuitable for it, derived from the practices of a male politics. Kathleen McCrone thus asserts that it was an 'irregular and unscientific' movement more concerned with bourgeois ascendancy than with women's rights.[8] It cannot be enough to dismiss it in those terms, though, for to do so denies the clear organizational autonomy and distinctive philosophy which the movement embraced.

The most obvious way in which the feminist distinctiveness of the women's movement in this period exhibits itself is in the conscious woman-centredness of its interests. Female identity, even if signalled through domesticity or purity, was a source of pride and identity, denying older prescriptions of shame and inferiority, and was manifested at a number of levels. Organizationally, the distance between feminist movements and other reforming groups demonstrates this distinctiveness. Frances Power Cobbe, whose prominence in a host of feminist campaigns throughout her life made her an important figure in the movement stoutly maintained that, 'ours is the old, old story of every uprising, race or class or order. The work of evolution must be wrought by ourselves or not at all'.[9] To some extent that bid for independence, for women's own assertion of their political capacities, was based on a purely pragmatic assessment of the situation.

Since when have one or two women's questions, more particularly those relating to education and property, been dealt with in the Houses of Parliament? Exactly since the time that women have banded themselves together to ask for votes with which to do their own work?[10]

It was a stand which went far beyond a relatively straightforward belief in the need to retain political control of their own organizations and destiny. There was, in addition, a conscious seeking out of female company among many women, married as well as single. Edith Simcox relates an anecdote in which her beloved friend, Mary Ann Evans – better known as the novelist George Eliot – upbraided her for this trait.

> She said . . . she believed I should have thought more of the adventure if a woman had been kind to me. I said I might have if I had had the opportunity of being kind to a woman. But that I had no prejudice whatever against men.[11]

Simcox was by no means unusual in her preference for female company. Many women felt severely their want of education in the company of men or found the barriers of separate sphere respectability forced conversation with them into topics of limited potential. Their relationships with other women held no such fears or fetters, and many chose companionship with women as a lifestyle preferential to marriage. Married feminists, too, frequently chose the company of women, and indeed their professional services as well. England's first home-trained woman doctor, Elizabeth Garrett, acted as physician to a number of feminists, among them Josephine Butler and Lady Kate Amberley. Garrett also ran a dispensary for women and children, founded in the wake of the cholera epidemic of the mid 1860s and staffed entirely by women.

> Women of the late nineteenth and early twentieth centuries gave each other strength to create myriad institutions; to attack male domination in every area of society, and to fight for legal, educational, political and social reforms with an effectiveness that we have yet to match.[12]

The extent of this network of female support at an emotional, intellectual and political level is, of course, not easy to measure. It is, however, interesting to note a criticism of it, made in 1926 by a woman whose principal experiences of the feminist movement had been in the last two decades of the nineteenth century and the very earliest years of the new century. 'For some time back we have been in danger of producing a type which finds its ideals in a world of women rather than in the world as it is.'[13] The point is an interesting one, because for all the pragmatism of their tactics, feminists were constantly critical of male conduct and male morality in all spheres. Their celebration of their own moral superiority derived much of its force from the contrast with the degradation they saw as a fixed point of reference in male political and sexual behaviour alike. Lady Frances Balfour was implicitly critical of that tendency in her praise of women's freedom from it.

No selfish jealousy ever marred any stage of the Women's Movement. . . . Through the whole of my experience, I never saw or heard any symptom of a jealous spirit; women had no temptation to fight for place, or honours.[14]

Balfour was from a political family. Her father was the Duke of Argyll, a prominent Whig, and she married the brother of Conservative politician and British Prime Minister, A. J. Balfour. She thus had ample opportunity to observe governing politics at close quarters, and her comments reflect the capacity of feminists to translate their politics on to a different plane.

Eugenia Palmegiano has noted that the mid-century movement had 'no acknowledged leader, no powerful organization, no official propaganda'.[15] In short, it failed to fit the pattern of orthodox and male political organizations. The argument that the women's movement was weakened by its relinquishment of the trappings of organizational conformity serves simply to highlight the failure of the historical imagination. Feminism did not fail to achieve these goals; it chose to reject them and with them the hierarchies of male political organization. The networks which offered solace and support within the feminist camp were an alternative politics. Leadership was diffused, and though there were prominent figures, no power struggles ever disfigured the movement, as Frances Balfour noted above.

Women desired political equality, then, but not on wholly male terms. Their use of the perceived differences between the two sexes as their major referent was a means of asserting their demands without incurring yet more hostility. Their claims for participation in public life would inevitably invoke opposition, but it was an opposition which could be, if not mitigated, at least subdued by their insistence on retaining the essential features of womanliness.

The question had been placed upon a broader basis, not woman's *rights*, as a middle-class spinster with a livelihood to fight for, against hostile male forces, but woman's *duties*, not only as a spinster, but also as a wife and mother.[16]

There were women within feminism who had learned their first political lessons at a young age. Many came from politically active families or had married men with political careers. Women such as the Ashurst sisters or Priscilla McLaren had been reared in an environment conducive to their future political interests. McLaren was the sister of politicians John and Jacob Bright and had absorbed her politics through organizations such as the Anti-Corn Law League in the early 1840s and through her Quaker associations. The four Ashurst girls – Emilie, Caroline, Matilda and Eliza – were the daughters of the radical lawyer William Ashurst and had been reared in an unusually liberal atmosphere. For the most part, however, women's route into feminism was not as clear-cut or simple. Most came from more ordinary backgrounds, though sometimes from families where religious non-conformity had perhaps prompted an early understanding of injustice and prejudice.

There were a few whose introduction to feminism came via their mothers. Fifty years in the life of a social movement is, after all, a long time, and in that period we can trace two or three generations of feminists taking an active part. Inevitably, a few of the younger women inherited a feminist tradition, mother to daughter. Among the most obvious successors to a maternal feminism were Philippa Fawcett, Millicent's daughter and Helen Taylor, daughter of Harriet Taylor-Mill. Millicent Fawcett's reaction to Philippa's outstanding academic success is an interesting one. Replying to the host of congratulatory notes that poured in when her daughter was placed high above the male candidates in the mathematics degree results at Cambridge in 1890, Millicent commented with moving simplicity:

The news on Saturday night made me very happy. You will know that I care for it mainly for the sake of women; but of course I also feel myself especially blessed in the fact that the thing I care most of all for has been helped on in this way by my own child.[17]

Hilda Martindale, who became a government factory inspector in 1901 (see Chapter 4), was brought up in an entirely female household. Her father, William Martindale, had died in 1874, some three years after his marriage, leaving his wife Louisa and two daughters, Louisa and the younger Hilda. In her memoirs, Hilda describes her mother's growing awareness of feminist arguments in the 1880s, reading feminist periodicals and seeking out like-minded women. She moved towns in order to gain access for her daughters to schooling run on feminist lines and Hilda remembers being taken to hear Josephine Butler and Annie Besant speak. 'We met other leading supporters of the Woman's cause.'[18]

Hilda's contribution to the movement was as a prominent woman civil servant for the duration of her working life, while her mother Louisa, a generation or so earlier, had found her political outlets through women's organizations of various sorts. She became president of the Brighton branch of the Women's Liberal Federation, and was active in societies as varied as the Women's Co-operative Guild (see Chapter 5) and the National Union of Women's Suffrage Societies (see Chapter 3). Both women sought to integrate their belief in women's capacities and women's freedom into their everyday lives; the generation that separated them was important, for the different approaches they took and the choices open to them give us a yardstick by which to measure the growth of feminist consciousness and the successes of the feminist enterprise.

The movement did change, of course, over the fifty years under scrutiny here, not only in the personalities who dominated it (or at least its historical face) but also in its appraisal of the most pressing issues of the day and the tactics employed in the fight. Barbara Taylor noted that the earliest of organized feminists were 'very cautious in [their] approach to all sexual matters'.[19] And yet by 1870 women campaigners had abandoned euphemism in their public assault on male sexual behaviour, speaking openly of venereal disease and of prostitution. And by the close of the century the moral purity campaigns which were the legacy of that era were certainly central to the feminist philosophy. Equally their strategies grew less and less dependent on the requirements of ladylike behaviour, though an element of that anxiety always remained. In the 1860s the prettiest and best-dressed women were carefully placed in the front row at meetings and Lady Balfour recalled in her old age how 'we were weak enough to treasure any good-looking supporter in our midst'.[20] By the mid 1870s, however, the movement was prepared to play an active role in securing a parliamentary candidate's failure at election time if his attitude to women was hostile. It was a tactic which, by the early years of the twentieth century, had become widespread.

The employment of the blackball tactic meant, of course, that for many women the movement was demanding that their feminism take precedence over other political allegiances. Women's groups within the main political parties operated very differently from the independent feminist groups. Though Liberal organizations such as the Women's Liberal Federation or even the neo-Conservative Women's Liberal Unionist Association which emerged in the wake of the Irish Home Rule controversy in the 1880s, were often pledged to encourage the party to enfranchise women, they still worked within the limitations of a party ethos which many women found distasteful. There were humorous moments, such as when the Conservative activist Frances Power Cobbe, acting in her capacity as secretary of the National Society for Women's Suffrage, approached the Primrose League (the women's auxiliary of the Conservative Party) as to their views on the question. Lady Borthwick replied for the League, 'declining to discuss the matter. The Executive Committee of the Ladies Grand Council cannot enter into questions of contentious politics.'[21]

The Primrose League's understanding of their distance from the political scene was, however, different in kind from that adopted by feminists. Where the League accepted their role within the political machinery, feminist rejection of that politics involved a critique of its operation. There was a keen awareness of how the double standard operated in such a context.

Men of every shade of party summon women to their assistance . . . and their support does not mean, as in former times, merely making up cockades and driving about in open carriages, but the drudgery of organization, the patient canvassing from door to door, and days of argument, of expostulation, and of all the heart-burning excitement of the election. . . . While competent to instruct voters in their duties, they are pronounced incompetent to give a vote themselves.[22]

Feminism, in this period, then, signalled the adoption of an alternative set of values. Although many of these still inevitably accorded with the class and the ideology in which these women had grown up, they none the less offered not a negative and reactive protest, but a celebratory and positive image consonant with the place which women demanded for themselves, both within that society and for changing it.

The following chapters are designed both to follow the histories of campaigns at their individual level and, at the same time, to provide a view of a more sustained political analysis running through the specific protests which ordered and made vocal the wider demands of a movement battling against entrenched power and privilege. Each chapter can be read as a discrete entity in itself, but the endless crisscrossing between campaigns outlined in the following pages argues against reading either this book or the women's movement in Victorian England in so fragmented a way.

Notes and references

1 Catherine Hall, 'The Early Formation of Victorian Domestic Ideology', in S. Burman (ed.), *Fit Work for Women* (London, 1979), pp. 15–32.

2 Penny Boumelha, *Thomas Hardy and Women: Sexual Ideology and Narrative Form* (Brighton, 1982), p. 5.

3 Millicent Garrett Fawcett, *Home and Politics* (London, n.d., ?1894), p. 3.

4 Fawcett Library, London. Autograph Letter Collection: Women's Movement, 1865–71. Helen Taylor to Barbara Bodichon, 7 August 1869.

5 Ross Evans Paulson, *Women's Suffrage and Prohibition. A Comparative Study of Equality and Social Control* (Illinois, 1973), pp. 26–7.

6 Marilyn J. Boxer and Jean H. Quataert, 'The Class and Sex Connection: An Introduction,' in their *Socialist Women. European Socialist Feminism in the Nineteenth and early Twentieth Centuries* (New York, 1978).

7 Jane Marcus, 'Transatlantic Sisterhood: Labor and Suffrage Links in the Letters of Elizabeth Robins and Emmeline Pankhurst,' *Signs* 3 (Spring, 1978), pp. 744–55 (p. 744).

8 K. E. McCrone, 'The Assertion of Women's Rights in Mid-Victorian England,' *Canadian Historical Association Historical Papers* (1972), pp. 39–53 (pp. 49–50).

9 Frances Power Cobbe, *The Duties of Women. A Course of Lectures* (2nd edition, London, 1882), p. 10.

10 Mary Ashton Dilke, *Women's Suffrage* (London, 1885), p. 26.

11 Bodleian Library, Oxford. MS Eng. misc. d. 494, *Autobiography of A Shirt Maker* (Edith Simcox), 9 November 1877.

12 Martha Vicinus, ' "One Life To Stand Beside Me": Emotional Conflicts in First Generation College Women in England', *Feminist Studies* 8 (1982) 3, pp. 603–28 (p. 625).

13 Janet E. Courtney, *Recollected in Tranquillity* (London, 1926), p. 132.

14 Lady Frances Balfour, *Ne Obliviscaris. Dinna Forget*, 2 vols, (London, 1930), II. 120.

15 Eugenia Palmegiano, 'Feminist Propaganda in the 1850s and 1860s', *Victorian Periodicals Newsletter* **11** (1971) pp. 5–9 (p. 5).

16 Enid Stacy, 'A Century of Women's Rights,' in Edward Carpenter (ed.), *Forecasts of the Coming Century by a decade of writers* (Manchester, 1897), p. 92.

17 Fawcett Library, London, Letters of Millicent Garrett Fawcett: Correspondence. Box 89, f. 16. Fawcett to Mrs Thursfield, 13 June 1890.

18 Hilda Martindale, *From One Generation to Another. 1839–1944. A Book of Memoirs* (London, 1944), p. 36.

19 Barbara Taylor, *Eve and the New Jerusalem* (London, 1983), p. 280.

20 Balfour, *Ne Obliviscaris*, II. 137.

21 Bodleian Library, Oxford, Papers of the Primrose League. Ladies' Executive Committee Minute Book, 1885–6, f. 62, 13 November 1885.

22 C. A. Biggs, *A Letter from an Englishwoman to Englishwomen* (London, n.d., ?1889), no pagination.

2 Education: the first step

The foundation of new educational opportunities for women was one of the major areas of the new feminist activity which emerged at this time. Women saw education as the key to a broad range of other freedoms; as a means of training for paid employment, as a means of alleviating the vacuity and boredom of everyday idleness and, of course, as the means to improving their ability to fight for the extension of female opportunities in a host of other areas.

Throughout this period, and even after the successful establishment of girls' schools and womens' colleges, arguments were aired which sought to prove the depredations consequent upon women's participation in education. The energy given over to mental exertion would affect their future capacity for reproduction; their presence would serve to unnerve both male students and teachers; their removal from an overriding concern with domestic matters would serve to undermine family life. 'Women who have stored their minds with Latin and Greek seldom have much knowledge of pies and puddings.'[1] And even where an acceptance of the need for a furtherance of women's educational chances was acceded, debates raged – even within the feminist camp – as to the nature of that education and how far it should conform to or differ from that prescribed for boys and men. We shall look at the motives behind these various arguments at a later stage, when we examine more closely the part played by education in socializing girls *and* boys into their ordained roles.

There were, of course, many girls' schools (though no womens' colleges in the tertiary sector) in existence prior to the outburst of energy which began in the late 1840s with the foundation of Queen's and Bedford Colleges for Ladies. The earlier fee-paying girls' schools – leaving aside church, factory and philanthropic ventures for the children of labourers – were essentially commercial enterprises, catering for a middle-class clientele and seeking at least nominally to recreate the ambience of family life. In consequence, they were very small establishments, rarely more than thirty or so students, where the accent was rather less on academic acquirement than on appropriately feminine accomplishments. When the Royal Commission on Secondary Education (the Taunton Commission), appointed in 1864, sought information on such schools from its women witnesses, their revelations added up to a grim catalogue of incompetence and ignorance.

Want of thoroughness and foundation; want of system; slovenliness and showy superficiality, inattention to rudiments; undue time given to accomplishments and those not taught intelligently or in any scientific manner; want of organisation.[2]

The dismissive conclusions reached by this all-male commission are upheld by the reminiscences of women who had attended such institutions. Astronomer Mary Somerville recollected her brief sojourn at a Scottish boarding school for girls where 'the chief thing I had to do was learn by heart a page of Johnson's dictionary'.[3] And writing her autobiography in the 1890s, Frances Power Cobbe maintained that:

. . . to inspire young women with due gratitude for their present privileges, won for them by my contemporaries, I can think of nothing better than to acquaint them with some of the features of school-life in England in the days of their mothers.[4]

Of her own expensive boarding-school education in Brighton in the 1830s, she commented acidly that, 'everything was taught us in the inverse ratio of its true importance'.[5]

Cobbe was correct in underlining the changes which had taken place in that half century or so. By the 1890s, universal elementary schooling had been in existence, legally at least, for two full decades, many new and academically competent private schools for girls had been founded, women's colleges in the University of London and the new civic Victoria University in Manchester were awarding degrees to women, and though neither of the two ancient universities – Oxford and Cambridge – were admitting women to degrees, women were none the less studying for and sitting their examinations within the precincts of the women's colleges. In addition, small numbers of women were facing the huge challenge posed by the male medical profession and could now train at women's medical colleges in London or Edinburgh established by the pioneer women doctors. Teacher training colleges for women were churning out efficient graduates and, though the battle was not yet won, these victories represented a major advance. Earlier generations of women had been essentially self-educated; the quest for knowledge, and the powers it was deemed to bring, were common feminist motifs. We find them reflected not only in the tracts of educational reformers but among women novelists of the period. George Eliot's constant reiteration of the thirst for knowledge and Charlotte Brönte's preoccupation with fictional teachers and governesses are just the most well-known. And their female characters accurately reflect the fact that, for the most part, women were principally self-educated.

One interesting example of the extraordinarily high motivation which characterized women's self-education is the case of Annie Rogers, whose efforts to obtain recognition for women at Oxford University were so important.[6] Though her formal education was conducted largely by governesses and by a few courses taken at the new School of Art established by John Ruskin in Oxford, Annie's performance in the Local Examinations conducted by the Examination Syndicate of the University were so good that she was offered an exhibition to study at Worcester College, an offer withdrawn when the college's governing body discovered her sex. The exhibition went instead to a male candidate who had been placed sixth to Annie's first in the examinations.

Future art historian and trade union organizer Emilie Dilke 'used to horrify her ordinary church friends by her studies in dissection and anatomy'.[7] In Oxford in the 1880s the first generation of academic wives organized informal women's lectures series on a variety of subjects.[8] In the absence of good formal tuition, women often organized their own education, either in small interest groups or alone. Education was more than simply an antidote to the boredom of female middle-class existence; ignorance spelt continued subordination where education posited the possibility of independence. It was a common cry of feminists at this time, and not simply with regard to education, that marriage was not the only or indeed necessarily the most desirable option facing women. 'I cannot believe that it is every woman's duty to marry, in the eyes of the world.'[9]

It is important to remember that, for the most part, both

discussion and extension of women's education was confined to the better-off sections of English society, and more particularly to the middle classes. Studies have shown that recipients of the new education were drawn largely from professional and business families, those class fractions where an increasing security of status and wealth encouraged expenditure on female education, but where that wealth was likely to be insufficient to support daughters not catered for economically by marriage.[10] There were thus practical as well as ideological and political reasons which fostered the success of these educational campaigns.

In the context of the rigid social divisions which ordered Victorian society so thoroughly, there was nothing unethical in the decision to cater only for delineated social groups. Indeed, to attempt to mix children from different classes was to court disapproval and severely limit growth. The experimental Portman Hall School, founded in 1852 by Barbara Leigh Smith (later Bodichon) and Elizabeth Whitehead (later Malleson) was unusual, and most campaigners were careful as to their choice of students. Dorothea Beale, principal of the Cheltenham Ladies' College, one of the earliest of the new foundations, told the Taunton Commissioners in 1866 that at her school 'none are admitted but the daughters of independent gentlemen or professional men'.[11]

Some authors have argued that the improvement in girls' schooling was consonant with a more general attempt at reforming secondary education and owed more to the attentions of government through bodies such as the Taunton Commission than to feminist lobbying.[12] That commission, however, was only prompted to widen its concerns to include girls' education by the efforts of feminists. When Emily Davies wrote first to Matthew Arnold exhorting him to seek the inclusion of girls' schools, his reply was a curt one: 'I can hardly think that the new Commission, with all it will have on its hands will be willing to undertake the enquiry into girls' schools as well as that into boys.'[13] Had Emily Davies and other feminists not pursued this neglect, the commission would thus have looked only at the state of boys' secondary education. The growing responsibility which the state took upon itself in the provision of education – evidenced by the Education Acts of 1870 and 1876, the former going some way to providing a national system of elementary education (though very haphazardly) and implementing elective School Boards, the latter attempting to impose compulsory attendance – did not, however, address in any practical or serious manner the problem of providing women's education.[14] The state's failure in this respect only served to widen an already enormous chasm between what was considered appropriate for the different classes of society. In effect, compulsory education meant that working-class girls attending state schools were educated principally to a domestic role, with classes in laundry, home management, needle skills and the like, while in the private sector a crop of feminist-inspired and feminist-managed schools offered middle-class girls a curriculum almost identical to that of their brothers. University reform in this period has a rather different history. The government commissions of the 1850s and 1870s, which investigated all aspects of the Universities of Oxford and Cambridge from revenues to undergraduate admission, made no mention of women's admittance. Feminist agitation was far more prominent than state intervention at the tertiary level.

Feminist principles had no impact on the syllabus laid down in state schools; the question of just how radical their intention was in the private sector has been another source of contention among historians. Carol Dyhouse and Sarah Delamont, in particular, have argued that women educational campaigners perhaps fit more readily into the camp of the liberal reform movement responsible for introducing universal elementary schooling than into an explicitly feminist mould.[15] They have argued that traditional notions of femininity were not challenged in these new establishments, which thus reinforced conventional sex roles rather than seeking to undermine them.

Certainly there were many who argued that the function of expanding the education of women was to fit them more adequately for domestic middle-class wife-and-motherhood. Writers such as John Ruskin felt that female education should take into consideration a husband's need to share *his* interests with his wife and conduct intelligent conversation with her.[16] In George Gissing's novel *The Odd Women*, cousin Everard is convinced that his friend's desertion of wife and child is fully justified on the grounds that his wife 'discoursed unceasingly of one subject – the difficulty she had with her domestic servants'.[17]

And there were others who propounded a moral reason for widening women's education. Millicent Garrett Fawcett, among others, explained the crucial role played by mothers in determining the early education of their infants.

The likelihood of a girl becoming a mother ought to be to her parents one of the strongest inducements to cultivate her mind in such a manner as to bring out its utmost strength, for upon every mother devolve the most important educational duties.[18]

None the less, Millicent's seemingly conservative thinking on this matter was qualified, and reflects more a shrewd understanding of women's common situation than a desire to perpetuate it.

Though it is important to show that higher education would fit women better to perform the duties of married life . . . the object of girls' education should be to produce, not good wives merely, but good women.[19]

Pauline Marks has suggested that educational activists can be divided into three categories: instrumentalists, whose goal was equality of opportunity; liberal humanists, for whom the function of female education was to fit them more properly for wife-and-motherhood; and moralists, whose chief interest was the inculcation of youngsters with Christian principles.[20] Educational reformers, feminist or not, were working within strictly bounded areas. The necessarily middle-class nature of the enterprise, concentrated on private schooling, forced some measure of caution and compromise upon them through their need to establish and maintain a paying clientele. Sarah Delamont's recognition of the double conformity this engendered – with the necessity to enforce both an appropriately ladylike code of behaviour and an acceptance of cultural values adopted from male definitions – is important.[21] The consciously academic profile and rejection of 'accomplishments' which characterized such schools regulated and disciplined their students to the values of the public world rather than the domestic sphere of the family. Janet Howarth has pointed out that they adhered to a far less exclusive policy than the equivalent boys' schools; neither the Headmistresses' Association founded by Frances Buss in 1874, nor the *Girls' School Year Book* which began publication in 1907, excluded local authority schools.[22] None the less, there clearly was an élite of girls' schools where academic achievement was highly prized, accompanied often by an encouragement to students to go on to higher education. It is in these schools that we can see the shaping hand of an explicit feminism.

In the late 1840s, in the wake of much public scandal over the plight of England's 25,000 governesses,[23] two women's colleges were founded in London, which were to play an important role as pioneer institutions. The first, founded in 1848 under the direction of Christian Socialist, Frederick Denison Maurice, was Queen's College, Harley Street, an Anglican foundation run principally by men sympathetic to the need for women's education. Queen's was soon followed by the Ladies' College, Bedford Square (which rapidly became known as Bedford College) in 1849. Bedford College differed from Queen's in a crucial respect; its founder was a woman committed not merely to the extension of educational provision for women but to granting them institutional autonomy. Elizabeth Jesser Reid wanted her college to be run by women and was careful to place the College's Trust in the hands of single women before she died in 1866.[24] Moreover, Elizabeth Reid was a Nonconformist, a member of the Unitarian faith from which so many nineteenth-century radicals emerged. Nonconformists felt sharply their exclusion from Anglican educational foundations and often made a point of funding non-denominational schools and colleges; the all-male Owen's College Manchester, was to fit the same pattern in the early 1850s.

Both Queen's and Bedford Colleges took girls of 12 years and upwards, and though their academic structure hinted at a higher education with their appointment of professors, they, in fact, fulfilled a rather less elevated need, providing a thorough if basic grounding for their students. Though Queen's College, directed entirely by men, can hardly be said to fit the feminist category, the radical structure of Reid's enterprise in Bedford Square, with its mixed governing body and preponderance of women, was a new departure. Its earlier supporters numbered many of the leading feminists of the day; Barbara Leigh Smith, Emily Davies, Elizabeth Blackwell, Emily Shirreff, Alice Westlake.[25] And together the two schools offered significant educational opportunity for active women; many of those who were to become active feminists in adult life received an education at either Queen's or at Bedford. Indeed, Diana Worzala has dubbed the two colleges 'academies of British feminism'.[26] In its early years Queen's graduates included educationalists Frances Buss and Dorothea Beale, early woman doctor Sophia Jex-Blake, and Frances Martin, who was subsequently to run the junior school attached to Bedford College. Women such as Bessie Rayner Parkes, Barbara Leigh Smith, Eliza Bostock, Anna Swanwick, the Cobden girls and Lady Noel Byron – all well-known women's activists – attended classes at Bedford College. And nor were these colleges providing only for younger women; a significant number of them attended at a relatively advanced age, further proof perhaps of the urgent need for competent women's schooling. Frances Buss was 21 years old and Adelaide Proctor 23 years old when Queen's College first opened, yet both were among its first students. It was not uncommon for radical families to send all their daughters to these colleges; whole families appear to have been in attendance simultaneously. The presence, throughout these years, of women who were to become prominent in feminist campaigns is an important determining factor when we seek to 'measure' the feminist input in educational reform at this juncture. Moreover, the staff of these new institutions were happy to champion the cause of women's education in specifically public ways; when Emily Davies memorialized (i.e. petitioned) the University of Cambridge to allow girls access to the new Local Examinations (see pp. 34–6) in October 1864, seventeen of the Queen's College staff and thirty-four of the Bedford College staff were signatories.[27]

It was not long before their impetus gave rise to more such enterprises; North London Collegiate School and Cheltenham Ladies' College, though as different in their aims as in their social composition, followed in the 1850s. Frances Buss was the eldest child of a respectable though by no means wealthy family, and began her teaching career at the age of 14. The North London Collegiate School had begun its life in 1845 as a fairly typical small private school, but after winning a diploma from the new Queen's College, where she was one of the first evening class students, Frances Buss remodelled the school along the lines of Queen's and it rapidly became an academic success story. From the start, however, its policies intimated only a partial incorporation of dominant values, exhibiting many of the characteristics with which feminist campaigners influenced these new schools. North London Collegiate School offered an academic education at a moderate cost – nine guineas per annum – to 'the families of professional men, the leading tradesmen and so on',[28] and though it was an Anglican school, pupils could opt out of religious education. One hundred and fifteen students were enrolled by the end of its first year. Cheltenham Ladies' College, while maintaining a similar commitment to academic rigour, had a more exclusive social status, seeing itself as the sister foundation to the male public school, Cheltenham College. Under Dorothea Beale, who reigned as principal from 1858 to 1904, the school rose to some considerable prominence. These two women espoused radically different philosophies of education, but their common devotion to the provision of girls' education and to its corollary, the creation of a competent female teaching profession, drew them together; when Frances Buss founded the Association of Head Mistresses in 1874, Dorothea Beale was its first president. Buss, in turn, sat on the Council of Cheltenham Ladies' College.

In the wake of their foundation, there was a lull in feminist agitation for girls' secondary education for a decade or so. It was not until the 1860s that public activity was once more resumed, but from that time on there was no break in the fight for women's education, in both the secondary and tertiary arenas. The 1860s saw the battle for women's entitlement to medical training and qualification, the establishment of links with the universities, a nod in the direction of evening classes for working women and, of course, governmental enquiry into the condition of girls' schooling.

It was in the wake of the Taunton Commission's findings that widespread secondary schooling for girls began to take shape in both the new state sector and in the private establishments. Prior to the setting up of the commission, however, Emily Davies had seen a potential campaign in this area with the introduction of university-organized exams aimed at providing middle-class boys' schools with a uniform yardstick of quality. The Local Examinations, as they were known, were run by syndicates attached to the universities of Cambridge and Oxford. It was to these bodies that Davies first suggested that girls be permitted to sit the examinations. Emily Davies was the youngest daughter of an Evangelical clergyman who had married Mary Hopkinson, a businessman's daughter, in 1823. Her childhood was typical; while her brothers were educated at Cambridge, the education she and her sister received 'answered to the description of that of clergymen's daughters generally'.[29] Emily, however, was not content with the life thus ordained for her, and from an early age became active in women's campaigns. Before her move to London in 1862, she had founded a local branch of the new Society for Promoting the Employment of Women in Durham and Northumberland and had attempted, under its auspices, to win approval for women to sit Church and Mechanics' Institute Examinations. Once established in London, she turned her attention to a whole series of women's campaigns, principally in education. She was Elizabeth Garrett's most ardent supporter and one of the prime movers in the attempt to persuade London University to expand its charter to include women in 1862. Her attack on the Local Examinations, begun in the same year, was a tactical move aimed at furthering her determination to win access for women to higher education.

The examinations would be worth having, tho' I do not care so very much for them in themselves, because I think the encouragement to learning is most wanted *after* the age of eighteen. It seems likely, however, that if we could get these examinations, it would be a great lift towards getting the University of London.[30]

Oxford were explicit in their refusal to allow women's participation in the Locals, while Cambridge offered a qualified interest in Davies' proposal. The mixed campaign committee she had established then sought support from the regional committees which administered the exams and, in late 1863, Cambridge agreed to conduct a trial run for girls. They were given only six weeks in which to organize themselves and find adequately prepared girls, and were fully aware that failure would wreck the whole scheme. 'We shall look unspeakably foolish if we have no candidates after all, and people won't understand the reason.'[31] In the event, they mustered ninety-one candidates, of whom only eight withdrew before the examinations. With the exception of Cheltenham Ladies' College, the new girls' schools all sent candidates. Dorothea Beale, a rather more conservative educationalist than some, disapproved of the scheme, but North London Collegiate School sent over a quarter of the total applicants, and both Queen's and Bedford sent a contingent. Even before Cambridge had agreed to examine the girls' papers, the campaigners had taken wise precautionary preparation.

Hundreds of boys have failed, especially in spelling, and the failures are considered the most conclusive evidence in favour of the scheme. The Bedford College people are doing what they can. They complain bitterly of the deplorable ignorance of the girls who come to them at fifteen and upwards. The previous years seem to have been almost thrown away.[32]

Another tactic which the committee used to encourage applicants was to pay their fees by subscription rather than by charging individual candidates as was customary.

The results of those examinations are, of course, well-known in educational history. In general, the performance of the female candidates was impressive, save in the area of arithmetic, where their failures were markedly worse than the male candidates. The significance of this failure lies mainly in the curricular reforms it catalysed at both North London Collegiate School and at Queen's. None the less, the general success of the venture secured the permanent establishment of the scheme in 1865, though it passed through the Senate of the University by a dangerously narrow majority of fifty-five to fifty-one. Cambridge's lead was followed by other universities; London instituted a special women's exam in 1868 (which Emily Davies described as having been offered 'a serpent when we asked for a fish, tho' we cannot pretend to believe that serpents are better for us'.),[33] Oxford opened its Local Examinations to women in 1870 and Edinburgh and Durham soon followed suit. It was not long before the female candidates in the Local Examinations outnumbered the male, a phenomenon which is hardly surprising given the scant alternatives open to the girls.

The success of this campaign had two longer term results; it was proof, in a small way perhaps, that women could undertake the rigours of academic testing without compromising their 'femininity' and it also, of course, underlined the need for a greater number of schools serving the more academically-oriented girl. It was thus that in 1871 the National Union for the Improvement of the Education of Women of All Classes – which rapidly became known as the Women's Education Union – was inaugurated. It owed its existence to the work of two sisters, Maria Georgina Grey and Emily Anne Shirreff. The Shirreff sisters were active not only in educational movements but in the suffrage campaign, in local politics and in philanthropic organizations. The union had a wide brief, both in its commitment to raising academic standards and increasing provision, and in its attempts to standardize and raise the status of women teachers. It offered a variety of financial incentives, financing teacher traineees through its Teacher Education Loan Committee and offering various scholarships to women students. The most ambitious and long-lasting of its activities though, was the foundation of the Girls' Public Day School Company, later the Girls' Public Day School Trust.

The company was established in the summer of 1872 with the intention of financing new girls' schools by selling shares in the company. The capital acquired through the initial sale of shares at £5 apiece was used to fund the actual setting up of the school, while any profits accruing from tuition fees went towards dividend payments. The schools charged moderate fees, offered an academic programme as well as physical education, provision for non-Anglican religious instruction, and insisted upon hiring only trained teachers. The project was an enormous success. The first school opened early in 1873 in London's Chelsea with a modest twenty pupils; by the end of their first decade, the company had established seventeen schools, with a total enrolment of over 2800 girls.[34]

The Chelsea school operated from 9.30 a.m. to 1.30 p.m. Monday to Friday, offering all its classes bar solo-singing and instrumental music for the fixed fee. In the preparatory department, the termly fee was two guineas. In the senior, it ranged from four to eight guineas depending upon the age at which a student entered. The fees were guaranteed for the duration of the pupil's stay and where families sent more than one of their daughters a 10 per cent reduction was made! The fee included supplies of school stationery, and lunch was also available for students. The tone set by the pioneer Chelsea school was to be followed by the subsequent foundations and certain crucial educational principles underlay their shared programme. No specific class exclusions were applied though the fees, however low, would have been beyond the reach of the larger proportion of the population. More importantly perhaps, the company did not rank ability by age. 'The gradations of the classes will be strictly in accordance with the ability of their pupils, and not according to their ages.'[35] Though the Women's Education Union was disbanded in 1882, the company continued to expand its operations and by the close of the century was administering more than thirty schools.

Alongside their work in the field of secondary education, the Shirreff sisters actively promoted the training of women teachers in accordance with the objectives of their Women's Education Union. A further foundation initiated by them under the nominal banner of the Women's Education Union was the Teachers'

Training and Registration Society founded in 1876 and establishing its first college – the Maria Grey Teachers' Training College – in 1879. The date is an interesting one, for it is also the year in which a bill to make teacher registration compulsory failed to pass through parliament, and in which the University of Cambridge set up a syndicate for teacher training which began examining in the following year.[36] The situation in teacher training mirrored that in schooling, however, where academic achievement was confined to the private and fee-paying institutions. Increasingly, the women teaching in the state elementary sector, who were generally working-class women, were effectively pushed out of the new teacher training schemes. The result was to divide education by both class and gender. Elementary education for working-class children was seen as requiring little more than child-minding skills, an appropriately female sphere, but not one for which training was seen to be necessary. M. E. David's distinction between educated and qualified middle-class schoolmistresses and certificated but not qualified working-class teachers is a useful abbreviation for this situation.[37] Both schools and their staff reflected the strength of class politics in Victorian England. None the less, within those narrow confines imposed by class, the relationship between the new secondary and the new higher education is only too obvious. An enormous number of the graduates of the new women's colleges took up a career in teaching. Of the 720 students who passed through Newnham College Cambridge between 1871 and 1893, just over a half went into teaching positions. At Girton, 123 of the 335 women awarded certificates there from its foundation until 1893 became teachers.[38] And nor was this the only way in which the tertiary sector fed the secondary sector. At Bedford College, scholarships from the Reid Fund made further study at Bedford available to students from the Frances Mary Buss schools. North London Collegiate students could compete annually for a two-year scholarship at the college. Camden School received a one-year scholarship for Bedford to the value of twenty guineas.[39]

By 1900, a host of other endowed and proprietary schools for girls had been established alongside those already mentioned. In the 1881 edition of Helen Blackburn's *Handbook for Women Engaged in Social and Political Work*, fifty endowed and twenty-nine proprietary girls' schools are listed for England, and as Sheila Fletcher has noted, the state was responsible for founding many more girls' schools after 1870 than was private enterprise.[40] The distinguishing mark of these government-inaugurated schools, however, was their tendency to encourage a syllabus designed to train girls in domestic skills. An Education Department Code of 1878 provided for compulsory domestic education for girls in the state sector.[41] In essence, this class distinction was thus once again clarified; working-class girls were trained in domestic skills, while a proportion of middle-class girls were offered at least a route out of that sphere. As Sarah Delamont has noted, this was a new development in girls' schooling. Earlier in the century, it was the middle-class institutions which had offered a sex-specific curriculum, training girls in feminine accomplishments, while the children of labourers received a cursory and rudimentary but rarely role-related grounding in basic skills. By the beginning of the twentieth century Delamont sees the situation reversed, with middle-class girls receiving a similar education to their brothers and working-class girls a principally domestic and thus 'womanly' training.[42] This class-based curricular change occurred at a time when government's role in the provision of secondary education was becoming significant in the wake of the 1870 Education Act.

Despite its seemingly laudable intentions to provide at least the germ of a national system of schooling which would embrace all children, the effect of the 1870 act was to widen the gap between the education of children from different classes. In tandem with the Endowed Schools Act of 1869, it gave impetus to the rise of many new fee-paying schools, and it was in these rather than in the new state schools that feminist philosophies could be applied. Domestic economy was never prominent in the curriculum offered in the new girls' schools. In part, this reflected the assumption that their girls would hardly need such skills, as their role would rather be the supervision of domestic staff; but perhaps more importantly, in rejecting these all-important symbols of femininity, as they had similarly repudiated the 'accomplishments' of an earlier generation, such schools were making a political statement. Their espousal of a highly academic syllabus together with an attention to physical education was more than an emulation of the male education system; it was a means of challenging assumptions about the mental and physical ineptitude of women. Their almost exclusive concentration on middle-class girls is hardly surprising and we should exercise some caution in damning nineteenth-century feminists for this. In the first place, given their political

disabilities, they were hardly likely to have been given any opportunity of influencing the educational policies of government and
were therefore restricted to the fee-paying sector. Moreover, the
ideology of the separate spheres was clearly aimed at and so much
more effective in middle-class circles that they were thus, in a
sense, attacking it at source.

There was some minor activity in feminist educational provision
for working-class women and girls. A Working Women's College
was established in London in 1864, modelled on the Working
Men's College founded a decade earlier. Frederick Denison
Maurice, who had been central to the setting up of the male
organization, was active in the women's project too, alongside
Elizabeth Whitehead Malleson, who had been the director of
Barbara Leigh Smith's coeducational experiment, Portman Hall
School. Ten years later, after some dissension over the wisdom
of coeducational classes, Frances Martin began a new College for
Working Women, which was later to be named after her. Though
there were plans in the late 1870s to amalgamate with the Working
Women's College in order to facilitate teaching on the new
University Extension scheme, the negotiations did not bear fruit
and the colleges remained separate for many years.[43] Feminist
activists, like male radicals, were frequently involved in teaching
in evening classes for working people, but at the organizational
level, little else was initiated by feminist campaigners.

The only other means by which women were able to influence
government – and thus working-class – schooling policy was
through membership of School Boards. In the 1870s, many women
took local government office, a new avenue of political participation opened to them after 1869. Women had at that date
become eligible for election to Poor Law Guardianship positions
and in 1870, after the passing of the Education Act, to School
Boards. Though local government activity was hardly the exclusive
province of feminists, many of them none the less added this
involvement to their existing commitments. The public nature
and competitive manner of election involved in this area was, in
important ways, antipathetic to prevailing notions of femininity,
but there were many women none the less prepared to run the
gauntlet of public derision. The second edition of Helen Blackburn's *Handbook for Women Engaged in Social and Political
Work*, published in 1895, lists 128 women elected on to English
and Welsh School Boards between 1892 and 1895. Many of those

who stood for election were active feminists, and many of them were concerned chiefly with the field of education; Emily Davies and Elizabeth Garrett were the first two women to sit on the London School Board and remained the only two until their resignation in October 1873.

We were willing to do our best, but when it is remembered that the Board has consisted of forty-seven gentlemen and two ladies, it will not be a matter of surprise that the two ladies have proved incapable of doing their half of the work.[44]

In the heavy and unremunerated workload associated with such positions,[45] School Board women were not dealing primarily with girls' schooling, but with the schooling of working-class children, both boys and girls. They were commonly allotted to suitably 'feminine' committees such as the Needlework Sub-Committee, but their brief was far wider and their energies necessarily concentrated on issues other than the particular education required for girls. Thus, though many of the women elected to such positions were active and committed feminists, their educational interpretation of that feminist perspective was rarely given effective voice at local government level, a problem exacerbated by their small numbers on the Boards.

Activities devoted to gaining access for women to higher education were, as with secondary schooling, confined almost exclusively to the private sector. Governments throughout this period initiated enquiries into the state of university education but considerations of women's entry into such institutions were never raised. The fight for women's higher education occasioned the opening up of a whole range of debates. Elizabeth Garrett's decision to train as a doctor raised issues in women's education far beyond the most obvious point of the reluctance of the medical profession to open its doors to women practitioners. Elizabeth Blackwell, an English woman who had acquired the necessary qualifications abroad, had succeeded in being placed on the British Medical Register in 1859 but had thereafter been forced to work in the United States. She returned to practise in England in 1869, by which time other women were, in tiny numbers, struggling to qualify. In the wake of Blackwell's success, the British Medical Association forbade the registration in England of doctors trained abroad, effectively excluding women, as they were also barred from training at home. Elizabeth Garrett's stand to acquire British qualifications was an important one; it not only challenged the British Medical Association's reaction to the Blackwell case and sought endless loopholes to combat their obstinacy, but inevitably raised the wider question of women's admission to universities and other institutions of advanced learning, their suitability for and proficiency in such studies. In turn, that opened questions as to the consequences of such education, the long-term implications of further education for women.

Educationalists in Victorian England fell into two distinct camps; those who favoured a broad general education, the 'liberal humanists', and those advocating a more specific vocational training, whom we might call the 'utilitarians'. Feminists were not alone in seeing education as a necessary first step to an expansion in the scope of women's employment. The entry of women into the professions – the middle-class end of the occupational spectrum – was one major reason for the demands for higher education, and medicine was merely one of the more publicly-fought and bitter of the battles waged to achieve recognition of women's rights to a public and professional existence. Elizabeth Garrett's assessment of the oppostion which women such as herself encountered was a shrewd one. 'One of the roots of the medical prejudice against women doctors is the fear that they should lower the price of medical work.'[46] The tendency in the manual labour sector for women's entry into an occupation to result in a deskilling and a lowering of wages was thus transferred to the middle-class workplace.[47]

Interestingly, though, much of the most vocal opposition came from male students affronted by the prospect of sharing their privileged milieu with women. When Elizabeth Garrett was successful in passing her first examination hurdle at the Middlesex Hospital in May 1861, the examiner wrote to her. 'May I entreat you to use every precaution in keeping this a secret from the students.'[48] Where male student hostility generally took the form of rowdiness or petitions to their tutors, the more formal academic opposition posed far greater problems. The first coterie of women medical students at the University of Edinburgh were forced to take legal action when the university, having accepted fee-paying women students in 1869, then denied them access to the clinical instruction necessary to qualify. The resultant legal battle was lengthy and messy, with appeal after counter-appeal upsetting each previous decision and allowing the university to prevaricate.

When it became clear that vicory there was some distance off, the practical alternative was the foundation of a training college specifically for women. This went ahead in London in October 1873 with fourteen students, and enlisting the tutorial capacities of qualifed and sympathetic men. The new London School of Medicine for Women did not, however, offer a total package of solutions; it could neither offer the requisite clinical portion of the training nor, as a body unrecognized by the medical profession, examine future doctors. It was the Irish College of Physicians and Queen's University, Belfast, which, in 1877, agreed to recognize the new school, thus finally allowing the Edinburgh women to qualify. Clinical instruction was won, though at considerable financial cost, when the Royal Free Hospital (where there were no male students to create a fuss) agreed to provide the London School of Medicine students with their clinical experience. The five year trial was so successful that not only did the Royal Free maintain its clinical role but dropped the punishing cash subsidy it had previously imposed.

In 1886, Sophia Jex-Blake, who had been the principal protagonist among the early Edinburgh women, returned there to found an Edinburgh Medical School for Women. Her continued involvement in the London project had been made difficult by the appointment of Elizabeth Garrett Anderson as Dean of the School in 1883; the two women were at temperamental odds and, not wishing to damage the cause, Sophia Jex-Blake's removal from the scene was a wise, if personally painful decision. Even with the foundation of a second medical school catering for women, numbers were small; but the publicity surrounding their efforts had brought the issue of women's higher education into high public, and even governmental profile. Their need to matriculate at a university in order to complete their medical degrees invariably raised the whole question of women's admission to degree courses. The initial campaigning for that privilege was centred around London University where first Jessie Meriton White, in 1856, and then Elizabeth Garrett, in 1862, had applied for leave to sit the matriculation exam. (Both applications were rejected, though Elizabeth Garrett's by only one vote.) The most effective work towards tertiary education for women was achieved, however, in Cambridge in the 1860s and 1870s under the guidance, in particular, of Emily Davies: ' . . . it was borne in upon me that the only way to meet the situation would be to found a new College'.[49] 'Briefly, the projected institution is to be, in relation to the higher class of girls' schools and home teaching, what the Universities are to the public schools for boys'.[50] From the first, Davies aimed high. Her educational philosophy incorporated an insistence that girls be placed on the same footing as boys, and be exposed to the same curriculum and testing, as had been the case with their inclusion in the Local Examinations. Davies argued, with some considerable force, that what we would now call positive discrimination would hinder the achievement of her objectives. She had long been wary of the 'special needs' argument; 'the moment you begin to offer special things, you claim to know what the special aptitudes are'.[51] While many other women educationalists agreed with her argument that male and female education should be assimilated, there were those prepared to accept specific women's papers as a first step to securing their higher education.

At the same time that Emily Davies was organizing the preliminary committee to establish her dream of a women's college, the success of Anne Jemima Clough's Liverpool-based North of England Council for Promoting the Higher Education of Women, founded in 1867, had once again raised the possibility of instituting examinations designed for women. The new organization was an early supporter of Davies' efforts at Cambridge, and indeed had formed fund-raising committees to help establish Girton. Before long, however, fundamental disagreements emerged with a number of the founding principles on which Girton College was to rest. In common with many feminists and educationalists, Clough was opposed to Davies' insistence on the retention of compulsory Greek and Latin. She thought the fees too costly and was suspicious, too, of the college's attachment to the Anglican church.[52] These divisions were to lead in time to the development of a separate campaign at Cambridge with the foundation of Newnham College at its centre. Clough was, of course, its first principal and when her North of England Council disbanded itself in 1875, it was to the library at Newnham that it donated its remaining funds.[53] Davies remained on cordial terms with this potentially rival organization but staunchly defended her position. She was fully aware of the seeming contradiction in wanting a common education but a *women's* college. 'You cannot artificially separate boys and girls, and then suddenly throw young men and women together at eighteen.'[54] Davies was as tactically wise as she was practical and was well aware of the public outcry which a coeducational stance would have engendered. She constantly sought to underline the respectability of her projects. Commenting on the membership of the women's college committee, she remarked that: ' . . . the list includes no one specially known as advocating the Rights of Women. It was felt to be important to put forward only such names as would be likely to win the confidence of ordinary people.'[55] In reality, she was not as conservatively cautious as such a comment might suggest; though she claimed her detestation of Radicals, and more especially of Radical women, her social circle was a distinctly feminist one, and Girton's first executive committee included Barbara Bodichon (née Leigh Smith), Charlotte Manning, Lady Stanley and Mrs Emilie Russell Gurney, all well-known feminists.

Her determination to maintain high standards of Victorian propriety were also reflected in her organization of the actual college. The college opened its doors to its first five students at a hired house in Hitchin near Cambridge in 1869 but Davies insisted upon the enactment of all the formalities of a traditional Cambridge college. When it moved to a purpose-built residence on the outskirts of Cambridge – to Girton village, from which it took its name – she had been careful to ensure that its design was along traditional collegiate lines, although at first no chapel was incorporated in the plans. However, in her insistence on common standards and in her willingness to accept non-Anglican students – two of the first five were Quakers – Davies' own radicalism is clear. In a sense, and ironically, it was Anne Clough, with her willingness to accept a separate syllabus and examination for women, who was conforming. 'She knew that women should not be expected to run, academically, before they could walk.'[56] Davies' uncompromising stand invariably involved her in endless wrangles with the governing bodies at Cambridge. For many decades the college was reliant on the goodwill of sympathetic dons willing to open their courses to Girton (and latterly Newnham) students and to mark their exam papers informally. Again and again as women students proved their abilities, appeals were made to regularize the curious anomaly of their unofficial presence, but to no avail. It was to be well into the twentieth century before Davies' views were vindicated by that success.

The situation at Oxford was rather different from that at Cambridge. Organization there began a few years later and was, for the most part, consciously non-feminist. While the campaigns at Cambridge had been spearheaded by women outside the existing academic community, at Oxford the active women were the daughters, sisters and wives of college fellows. 'It has been a domestic matter, and there has never been occasion to appeal to a wider public . . . or to apply pressure from outside.'[57] In 1878 an Association for the Higher Education of Women in Oxford was founded. It was far more than a pressure group; it administered a range of lecture courses for women and provided, through subscription and donation, halls of residence for women coming to Oxford to study. Its first two residences opened in 1879; Lady Margaret Hall and Somerville College. In effect, their activities constituted the establishment of a parallel collegiate system for women but one with no official university recognition. From 1884, the university had permitted the Local Examinations Delegacy (the equivalent of the Local Examinations Syndicate at Cambridge) to admit women to degree examinations but with no consonant recognition of their results. In opening both tuition and examination to the women's colleges and yet offering them no formal membership of the university, the authorities at Oxford were responding to a situation different in kind from that at Cambridge, where a far higher public profile had been engineered by the women campaigners. One of the early Oxford women students brought out their tactical and ideological differences in her description of her days at Somerville College. 'It was the spirit of unobtrusive receptivity and deference to University traditions and prejudices rather than a demand for rights which the Principal, Miss Shaw Lefevre, took pains to instil into the first students.'[58] The situation at Manchester was similarly informal, women having been admitted in 1875 to various classes at Owen's College, but as visitors rather than as fee-paying students. When, in 1877, a Manchester and Salford College for Women was established, many of the staff of Owen's College taught there though no formal connection ever existed between the two institutions.

Organizationally, then, as Gillian Sutherland has remarked, the years between 1869 and 1880 'saw activity more intense than at any other time in the century' in establishing focuses for the provision of female education.[59] The existence, however, of schools and colleges does not in itself constitute proof of feminist input; as we have seen, there were women at that time who dissociated their educational activities from feminism, as there are latter-day historians who would argue that the general tenor of social reform which marked the dominant liberalism of this period was a more forceful factor than feminist agitation in securing such provision. However, the educational philosophies which activated many of the institutions described offered considered alternatives to the type of education offered at this juncture in important and – I would argue – distinctly feminist ways. For the most part, women's educationalists derived their thinking from a practical combination of existing ideas and a consideration of the particular needs of women. The increasing need for and indeed desire of many women to earn their own livelihood had both set in train campaigns around expanding the scope of women's employment opportunities and focused much of the educational practice. Though campaigners such as Emily Davies embraced much of the culturally dominant mode of male education, they rarely adopted its whole thinking uncritically. The argument that the education of boys and girls should not be segregated was explained in terms of the inability of educationalists to decide upon what constituted a correct education. Women witnesses before the Taunton Commission reiterated that point over and over. Frances Buss, championing an equivalent education for both sexes, noted that 'it is rather difficult to ascertain what is the proper education for a boy'.[60] And Emily Davies' rejection of a separate girls' syllabus was based on a similar reasoning. Ironically, it was an identical, though perhaps more developed, dissatisfaction with prevailing educational values which had motivated the other camp into acceptance of an alternative syllabus. Both at Oxford and at Newnham, Cambridge, arguments against accepting the existing curriculum were based on the effect that this would have in strengthening and entrenching a narrow and outdated set of educational values to which the reformers could not adhere.

It was not only the syllabus offered in schools and universities which came under fire; the competitiveness of the dominant system was also attacked. In her submission before the Schools Inquiry (Taunton) Commission, Frances Martin argued that it was 'injurious to boys just as much as to girls. I think it fosters vanity and self-will in boys as well as girls.'[61] And Emily Davies saw herself as 'directly working towards preserving women from becoming masculine in a bad sense'.[62] This was not a ruse to preserve femininity but a direct and critical understanding of the problems associated with the values of male public life.

The London examinations do not strike me as eminently suitable either for men or for women, but . . . so long as this arbitrary dictation of studies goes on, we have no chance of finding out what women would choose, if they had a free choice.[63]

While adopting for the most part the *academic* values of Victorian education, the new women's institutions rejected much of the associated baggage. In religious terms, they tended, as we have seen, to be non-denominational in practice even if conforming outwardly to Anglicanism, and their rejection of the harsh and competitive regime imposed in, for instance, the growing boys' public schools of the day lent them a distinctive radicalism.

Both the campaigns and the schools and colleges which succeeded them were constrained to some extent by the practical and pragmatic need to attract a paying clientele and sustain some measure of influential support. The attitude of the feminists to their male supporters strongly suggests that the women understood in clear terms the necessity for tactical modification of their visions on occasion. There is an amused tolerance in Emily Davies' description of the male supporters of her early women's college committee.

Mr Clay and Mr Tomkinson were almost too strong on our side and too determined to make the College a paradise. They insisted that the girls should have breakfast in their own rooms (instead of all together like a school) as if the whole thing depended upon it. . . . [64]

And yet at the same time, they had no choice but to use all the weapons of persuasion in their power. As Elizabeth Garrett remarked:

I am glad they cannot say I am masculine, it is a providence that I am small and unangular. For the same reason I am very careful to dress well habitually, rather more richly in fact than I should care to do if I were not in some sort defending the cause by doing so.[65]

Their care in attention to detail was not, of course, always successful and the hostility which many of these women faced alone must have been galling. Another of the lone medical pioneers, Miss Colborne, described in a letter to Emily Davies her experiences in attempting to attend a lecture in physiology.

> . . . as the lecturer was explaining something when I entered, he did not discover me until the looks and coughs of the students had attracted his attention to my corner – he broke off in his lecture, and said he should like to decide whether the lecture should be continued or not, there was a show of hands against the continuance, the lecturer then bowed, pronounced the lecture discontinued, and the students left the room. I intend to try the Chemistry lecture tomorrow morning.[66]

In such circumstances it is hardly surprising to see counsel after counsel advising that the public face of the campaigns be promoted as reasonable and respectable.

> I find nothing irritates men so much as to attribute tyranny to them. I believe many of them do really mean well. . . . Men cannot stand indignation, and tho' of course I think it is just, it seems to me better to suppress the manifestation of it. I should not mind *saying* a few indignant things . . . but these papers travel about the country and so into families, where they may be read by prejudiced men. So it is necessary to be careful.[67]

Effectively, this problem meant that while the women were prepared to use men as figureheads to support their campaigns and to gain access for them to otherwise closed political channels, there developed at the same time a strong sense of female collectivity and difference. In part, it was a response to the kinds of hostility and ridicule they so frequently encountered and to the misunderstandings that even their male sympathizers exhibited, and in part an obvious pooling of their common experience of subjugation. In practice, this feature of feminist politics produced not only a country-wide network of feminist culture but had important ramifications in a professional context which links it back both to questions of education and of employment.[68]

In effect, the political upshot of these compromises was to ensure that little activity was undertaken outside the middle classes. Their concentration on the private sector, their need to maintain a 'moderate' profile as far as possible, their accent on academic excellence, were all factors which inhibited the percolation of these ideas down the social scale. By the turn of the century, the new feminist-inspired girls' schools were the major sources feeding the new women's colleges at Oxford and Cambridge. Janet Howarth has shown the predominance of Girls' Public Day School Company and public day schools such as North London Collegiate School in providing women students for the new colleges, and Joyce Pedersen's work has shown the matching class backgrounds of girls at such schools and colleges. From their foundation to 1894, the Oxford and Cambridge women's colleges show 64 per cent of students (of known origin) from professional backgrounds and 25 per cent from business families.[69] And that class orientation is nowhere made more obvious than in Mabel Tylecote's account of the early women students at Owen's College Manchester, whose only access to the college library in the 1890s was through servants.

We had to 'fill up a voucher', and a dear little maid-of-all-work, aged about 13, went to the library with it. If we were not quite sure of the volume required, she might have to make the journey ten times, but it was never suggested that she should be chaperoned.[70]

By the turn of the century, then, feminist educational thinking – whatever its class limitations and these should not be ignored – had established for itself an institutional focus in the new breed of girls' schools and in the new women's colleges. It was a movement aimed for the most part neither at the highest nor the lowest segments of this rigidly stratified society but at the growing middle classes where the vagaries of the economy were seen as more likely to push unprepared and untrained young women into the labour market.

Notes and references

1   Sarah Sewell, *Women and the Times we Live In* (London, 1868), quoted in Janet Horowitz Murray, *Strong-Minded Women and Other Lost Voices from Nineteenth Century England* (Harmondsworth, 1984), p. 213.
2   House of Commons, Parliamentary Papers 1867–8, XXVIII, Report of Schools Inquiry Commission, Ch. VI, Girls' Schools, p. 548.

3 Martha Somerville (ed.), *Personal Recollections: From Early Life to Old Age of Mary Somerville* (London, 1874), p. 22.

4 *Life of Frances Power Cobbe By Herself*, I (London, 1894), p. 58.

5 *Life of Frances Power Cobbe*, I, p. 64.

6 Annie M. A. H. Rogers, *Degrees by Degrees. The Story of the Admission of Oxford Women Students to Membership of the University* (Oxford, 1938), pp. 3–5.

7 British Library Add. MS. 43946. Dilke Papers, LXXIII. Charles Dilke's memoir of his wife, Lady Emilie Dilke (typescript), p. 14.

8 Oxford and Cambridge had only removed the bar on college fellows marrying in 1882; prior to that date, all fellows were required to be ordained and unmarried.

9 Josephine Butler, *Woman's Work and Woman's Culture. A Series of Essays* (London, 1869), p. xxxv.

10 See, for instance, the work of Joyce Pedersen, 'The Reform of Women's Secondary and Higher Education: Institutional Change and Social Values in Mid and Late Victorian England,' *History of Education Quarterly* (Spring 1979), pp. 61–91.

11 House of Commons, Parliamentary Papers, 1867–8. XXVIII. Report of Schools Inquiry Commission, Part V, Minutes of Evidence, 19 April 1866.

12 e.g. Carol Dyhouse, *Girls Growing Up in Late Victorian and Edwardian England* (London, 1981); Gillian Sutherland, 'The movement for the higher education of women; its social and intellectual context in England c. 1840–1880', in Philip Waller (ed.), *Political and Social Change in Modern Britain: Essays presented to A. F. Thompson*, forthcoming, 1987.

13 Girton College, Cambridge, Emily Davies Papers. Family Chronicle, f. 392. Letter to Acland, 28 December 1864.

14 Sheila Fletcher, *Feminists and Bureaucrats. A Study in the Development of Girls' Education in the Nineteenth Century* (Cambridge, 1980).

15 Dyhouse, Sarah Delamont, 'The Contradictions in Ladies' Education,' pp. 134–63, and 'The Domestic Ideology and Women's Education', pp. 164–87 in S. Delamont and Lorna Duffin (eds), *The Nineteenth Century Woman: Her Cultural and Physical World* (London, 1978).

16 John Ruskin, 'Of Queens' Gardens,' in *Sesame and Lilies* (London, 1865).

17 George Gissing, *The Odd Women* (reprinted, London, 1968), p. 81.

18 Millicent Garrett Fawcett, 'A Short Review of that Portion of the Report of the Schools Inquiry Commission which refers to Girls' Education', in Henry and Millicent Fawcett, *Essays and Lectures*

on Social and Political Subjects (London, 1872), VIII, pp. 185–205 (p. 202).

19 Fawcett, *Essays and Lectures*, p. 204.

20 Pauline Marks, 'Femininity in the Classroom: An Account of Changing Attitudes', in Mitchell and Oakley (eds), *The Rights and Wrongs of Women* (Harmondsworth, 1976), pp. 176–98, (p. 185).

21 Sarah Delamont, 'The Contradiction in Ladies' Education', p.140.

22 Janet Howarth, 'Public Schools, Safety-nets and Educational Ladders: the classification of girls' secondary schools, 1880–1914', *Oxford Review of Education*, **11** (1985) 1, pp. 59–71 (p. 60).

23 M. Jeanne Peterson, 'The Victorian Governess: Status Incongruity in Family and Society', in Martha Vicinus (ed.), *Suffer And Be Still. Women in the Victorian Age* (London, 1980), pp. 3–19.

24 Her insistence on the Trust being in the hands of *single* women reflects the legal minority of married women whose property was by right ceded to their husbands on marriage. See Chapter 6.

25 Beford College, Reid Papers GB 112/4/1. Elizabeth Blackwell was the first woman to qualify as a doctor. Emily Shirreff was one of the founders of the Girls' Public Day School Company and Alice Westlake was active in local government.

26 Diana Mary Chase Worzala, 'The Langham Place Circle: The Beginnings of the Organised Women's Movement in England, 1854–70', unpublished PhD. thesis, University of Wisconsin-Madison, 1982, p. 74.

27 Barbara Stephen, *Emily Davies and Girton College* (London, 1927), p. 98.

28 PP, 1867–8, XXVIII. Report of Schools Inquiry Commission, V. Minutes of Evidence 30 November 1865.

29 Girton College, Cambridge, Emily Davies Papers. Family Chronicle, f. 65.

30 Stephen, *Emily Davies and Girton College*, p. 83. Emily Davies to A. D. Richardson, 12 July 1862.

31 Girton College, Cambridge, Emily Davies Papers. Family Chronicle f. 319. Davies to Richardson, 26 October 1863.

32 Emily Davies Papers, f. 304. Davies to Richardson, 20 June 1863.

33 Quoted in Stephen, *Emily Davies and Girton College*, pp. 102–3.

34 Edward W. Ellsworth, *Liberators of the Female Mind. The Shirreff Sisters, Educational Reform and the Women's Movement* (Westport, Connecticut, 1979), p. 191.

35 'Introduction', *Journal of the Women's Education Union*, **I** (15 January 1873), p. 15.

36 Ellsworth, *Liberators of the Female Mind*, p. 206.

37 M. E. David, *The State, the Family and Education* (London, 1980), p. 125.

38 Alice M. Gordon, 'The After-Careers of University-Educated Women', *The Nineteenth Century. A Monthly Review*, XXXVII (1895), pp. 955–60 (p. 956).

39 Mary Gurney, *Are We To Have Education for Our Middle Class Girls?, or The History of Camden Collegiate Schools* (London, 1872), pp. 14; 21.

40 Fletcher, *Feminists and Bureaucrats*, p. 171.

41 Dyhouse, *Girls Growing Up*, p. 89.

42 S. Delamont, 'The Domestic Ideology and Women's Education', p. 164.

43 I am grateful to Liz Stanley for untangling the information on this for me.

44 Stephen, *Emily Davies and Girton College*, p. 27.

45 For a description of this, see Ethel E. Metcalfe, *Memoir of Rosamund Davenport-Hill* (London, 1904).

46 Girton College, Cambridge, Emily Davies Papers. Family Chronicle, f. 496. Elizabeth Garrett to Davies, 21 September 1866.

47 See Chapters 4 and 5 for details on women and employment.

48 Quoted in E. Moberley Bell, *Storming the Citadel. The Rise of the Woman Doctor* (London, 1953), p. 53.

49 Girton College, Cambridge, Emily Davies Papers. Family Chronicle, f. 500 (1866).

50 Quoted in Stephen, *Emily Davies and Girton College*, p. 52.

51 Girton College, Cambridge, Emily Davies Papers. Family Chronicle, f. 472. Davies to W. H. Hutton, n.d., 1866.

52 Blanche Athena Clough, *A Memoir of Anne Jemima Clough* (London, 1895), pp. 153–4.

53 Clough, *A Memoir*, p. 134.

54 Barbara Stephen, *Emily Davies and Girton College*, pp. 202–3. Davies to A. D. Richardson, 31 January 1868.

55 Girton College, Cambridge, Emily Davies Papers. Family Chronicle, f. 519 (1867).

56 Rita McWilliams-Tulberg, *Women at Cambridge. A Men's University – Though of a Mixed Type* (London, 1975), p. 58.

57 Annie M. A. H. Rogers, *Degrees by Degrees*, p. 2.

58 Lilian M. Faithfull, *In the House of My Pilgrimage* (London, 1924), p. 53.

59 Gillian Sutherland, *Politics and Social Change*, p. 3.

60 PP, 1867–8, XXVIII, Schools Inquiry Commission, Part V, Minutes of Evidence, 30 November 1865, Frances Mary Buss.

61 Schools Inquiry Commission, 21 March 1866.

62 Quoted in Stephen, *Emily Davies and Girton College*, p. 83. Davies to A. D. Richardson, 12 July 1862.

63 Stephen, *Emily Davies and Girton College*, p. 104. Davies to W. H. Hutton.

64 Stephen, *Emily Davies and Girton College*, p. 157. Davies to Barbara Bodichon, 6 April 1867.

65 Quoted in Diana Mary Chase Worzala, 'The Langham Place Circle,' pp. 249–50.

66 Girton College, Cambridge, Emily Davies Papers, Family Chronicle, f. 434. Miss M. Colborne to Davies, 7 November 1865.

67 Stephen, *Emily Davies and Girton College*, p. 108. Davies to Bodichon, 14 November 1865.

68 See Chapter 5 for a fuller discussion of these points.

69 Janet Howarth, 'Public Schools', pp. 70–1; J. S. Pedersen, 'The Reform of Women's Secondary and Higher Education', p. 77.

70 Mabel Tylecote, *The Education of Women at Manchester University, 1883–1933* (Manchester, 1941), pp. 32–3.

Chronology

1848 Queen's College founded.

1849 Bedford College founded.

1850 North London Collegiate School founded.

1852 Portman Hall School founded.

1854 Cheltenham Ladies' College founded.

1856 London University rejects a petition demanding women's admission to matriculation examinations.

1858 Elizabeth Blackwell's name is placed on the British Medical Register.

1863 Women sit Cambridge Local Examinations for the first time.

1864 Schools Inquiry Commission (Taunton Commission) set up. Working Women's College founded.

1865 Cambridge Local Examinations thrown open to women officially.

1866 Durham Local Examinations opened to women.

1867 North of England Council for Promoting the Higher Education of Women established.

1868 Report of Schools Inquiry Commission published. London University's first womens' examinations.

1869 Hitchin (later Girton) College opened. Endowed Schools Act. First women medical students at Edinburgh University.

Lectures for women established at University of Cambridge.

1870 Merton Hall (later Newnham College) opened.
First elections to School Boards; four women elected.
Oxford Local Examinations opened to women.

1871 Camden School founded.
College for Working Women founded. National Union for Improving the Education of Women of All Classes (Women's Education Union) founded.

1872 Girton College, Cambridge incorporated.
Girls' Public Day School Company founded.
Slade School of Art opened to women.

1873 First GPDSC school opened, Chelsea.
Journal of Women's Education Union founded.
Bishop Otter Memorial Training College for Schoolmistresses founded.

1874 London School of Medicine for Women founded.
Association of Head Mistresses founded.

1875 Newnham Hall, Cambridge established.
Medical Acts Amendment (College of Surgeons Act) – empowered College to admit women to examinations.
Elizabeth Garrett wins membership of British Medical Association.

1876 Manchester New College opened to women.
Medical (Qualification) Act – allowed for granting of qualifications to suitably qualified applicants regardless of sex.

1877 Trinity College, London opened its musical examinations to women.
Royal Free Hospital admits women to clinical instruction.

1878 New charter of University of London admits women.
Association for the Higher Education of Women in Oxford founded.

1879 Somerville Hall, Oxford founded.
Lady Margaret Hall, Oxford founded.

1880 Newnham Hall incorporated as Newnham College, Cambridge.

1881 University of Cambridge admits women to Honours examinations, though granting them certificates of proficiency and not degrees.

1882 Westfield College, London founded.

1884 Coeducational Victoria University, Manchester opened.

1885   Hughes Hall, Cambridge (teacher training) founded.

1886   Royal Holloway College, London founded.
        St Hugh's College, Oxford founded.
        Edinburgh School of Medicine for Women founded.

1893   St Hilda's College, Oxford founded.
        Oxford University abolishes chaperonage for women attending
lectures.

1894   Royal Commission on Secondary Education (Bryce
        Commission) – three women serve on Commission.

3   The public sphere: politics, local and national

Women's interest in securing access to political rights was not limited to the campaign for parliamentary suffrage; the growing powers acceded to various levels of local government in this period also attracted their keen attention and in the area of local politics women were to play a prominent role as early as the 1870s. Their gains in that dimension of the political scene fuelled both their determination to extend the right to vote to the parliamentary context and the strength and logic of their arguments.

So confident were the early women pioneers of the consistency and good sense of their case that they assumed – unlike their prophesies in other areas of women's struggles – a speedy success to their efforts.

The question of Woman Suffrage is, in principle, practically gained; it cannot be long before that principle will be established by the formal act of the Legislature. . . . We have on our side justice and common sense, and these two are enough to win the battle.[1]

The confidence expressed in 1874 was to receive some sharp setbacks through the ensuing years of the century, and the buoyancy of the early campaigns, though none of their determination, experienced some deflation. Writing at the close of the century, Elizabeth Wolstenholme Elmy wrote to her lifelong friend and co-activist Harriet McIlquham, 'Unless a great effort be made now, I do not believe you or I, or persons twenty years our junior, will live to see Women's Suffrage established in England.'[2]

Her judgement was largely correct, though there were a handful of ageing women in 1919 who could trace the movement's long history.

As a girl I was present at an obscure meeting in Bristol . . . and at last in 1919 – it seemed almost like a culmination in bathos – I dropped a little paper, on which I had placed a cross, into a ballot-box.[3]

The first organized suffrage committee met in 1866; forty-two years were to elapse before the parliamentary citadel gave way. The political wing of the feminist movement should not, however, be seen as a failure for its lack of immediate success in securing this end. The municipal franchise granted to single rate-paying women in 1869 and gradually extended over the following three decades was exploited to the full, offering women not only the experience of government but a growing conviction of their capacities and value. Millicent Garrett Fawcett who, as leader of the National Union of Women's Suffrage Societies (NUWSS), was associated pre-eminently with parliamentary concerns, was fully aware of the significance of women's gains in local government.

When some people make the assertion that we worked for Women's Suffrage for nearly fifty years without making any progress, they forget these things that were really of the utmost importance in paving the way for victory in wider areas.[4]

Historians have tended to see the struggle for the vote as the dominating feature of both nineteenth- and early twentieth-century feminism. It is certainly true that many feminists saw recognition of women in the parliamentary environment as the most effective means of securing juster legislation, and the vote itself as a symbol of that recognition. It was a campaign, though, which was accorded no greater attention than many of the other campaigns whose histories are recorded here. There was an obvious and logical consonance between this and other feminist claims as countless commentators pointed out.

If women had possessed votes during former administrations, undoubtedly the Contagious Diseases Acts would not have been imposed without a struggle, and the Factory Acts would have been submitted to a more thorough and impartial criticism.[5]

The organized feminism of the Victorian era did not begin its campaigning years on the suffrage issue; it was a full ten years after the establishment of the first married women's property committee (see Chapter 6) that the first suffrage committee was born. The granting of the vote was an obvious area of feminist concern but by no means the overriding one. It was also one of the areas of least success for the movement, at least in the short term, which suggests perhaps that the legislators rather than the protesters saw it as crucial. The constant denial of the franchise to women at a time when feminist campaigns were enjoying success in a host of other areas – education, the opening of the professions, married women's property, the double standard – sets it apart not as their dominant concern but as the demand which men were not willing to concede.

Feminists approached the demand for the vote with a broad range of reasoning. Their specifically political arguments centred upon the issues of equality and representation, while their ethical arguments extended from a simple declaration of justice to a belief in woman's moral superiority and fitness. The views of women in the various suffrage organizations – and it was an issue which spawned a large body of societies – differed considerably, and on this, more than any other issue, profound political disagreements emerged within the feminist world. In the early 1870s, some women voiced concern over the growing proximity of their work with that of the prostitution regulation repealers (see Chapter 6). The resulting schism was only the first of three such upheavals; another occurred in 1888 over an issue of similar principle and there was further and severe disharmony over the precise terms on which the vote was being demanded. As Barbara Caine has pointed out, 'Almost every other specific objective of the nineteenth century women's movement was gained more quickly, with greater ease and with considerably less unpleasantness and hostility than was the vote.[6]

The gaining of the franchise, of course, pointed to potential alignment with existing political parties and some of the disagreement arose from a sense of political friction. Feminist societies throughout the period always maintained their distance from adherence to mainstream politics, criticizing Liberal and Conservative governments alike for their entrenched attitudes to women. Many feminists did, of course, profess political beliefs which coloured their feminist leanings, but for the most part women of vastly differing political hue worked harmoniously together. The specifically political nature of this campaign, however, made it the inevitable site of their discord. When changes occurred in the very earliest London suffrage committee of which Emily Davies disapproved, she remarked to her friend Anna Richardson, 'It is a great relief to me to get away from uncongenial companionship and to abandon the vain effort to work with

Radicals.'[7] And yet the new committee which Emily Davies so deplored for its radical taint included both the Liberal Millicent Fawcett and the Conservative Frances Power Cobbe on its executive, alongside the Radical wing represented by Clementia Taylor.

The various grounds on which women claimed their right to the parliamentary franchise represents the entire spectrum of political opinion and rehearses the contradiction between the reality of women's powerlessness and the political philosophies proclaimed at the time. For many women, this understanding led them to a surprisingly uncritical acceptance of the property terms of the Victorian franchise, though they argued at the time that the acceptance of a restricted franchise was a matter more of expediency than of principle. 'Half a loaf is better than no bread', as Millicent Fawcett told her young cousin Edmund.[8] And as she wrote in a more public context, 'The suffrage has not been claimed for women in England as an abstract and inalienable right, but it has been claimed upon the ground of expediency.'[9] Fawcett was voicing an acknowledgement of existing conditions more than an unyielding feminist principle; voting was by no means an inalienable right but one granted only to those whose proof of good citizenship could be weighed by the contents of their purse or the amount of their property. The justice and equality which the earliest generation of feminist suffragists claimed was no more than equality with men, with existing arrangements.

As long as the Parliamentary Suffrage is based on certain property qualifications, none who fulfil those qualifications ought to be excluded from the list of voters. This principle is maintained in our law with the most undeviating rigidity in all cases except in that of women.[10]

Fawcett was not concerned here with the merits or otherwise of the system, but more with the illogicalities it entailed. It was a position which, none the less, led the largely middle-class constituency of feminism into asserting their rights as a class as distinct from a sex.

That a respectable, orderly, independent body in the state should have no voice, and no influence recognized by the law, in the election of the representatives of the people, while they are otherwise acknowledged as responsible citizens, are eligible for many public offices, and required to pay all taxes, is an anomaly which seems to require some explanation.[11]

Conservative women, more particularly, leapt upon the contrast between the exclusion of middle-class women and the gradual extension of voting rights to working men, to what Cobbe called 'a rabble of illiterates'.[12]

To individual men the law says, 'All of you whose rental reaches the proscribed standard shall have your political existence recognized. You may not be clever nor learned; possibly you do not know how to read and write . . .'

But to individual women the law says, 'It is true that you are persons with opinions, wants, and wishes of your own . . . and that your intelligence is not inferior to that of great numbers of male voters . . . but . . . we will not allow you to have the smallest share in the government of the country.'[13]

None the less, even Conservative women were not unaware of the ramifications of their demand. It was a constant cry of women campaigners that withholding the franchise from women made nonsense of Britain's claims to be a nation of representative government. It was their contention that elected members would naturally represent, for the most part, the interests of their own kind, a view which suggests that feminists took a dim view of politicians and their behaviour. 'Can it be believed for a single moment that if women had had any share in the making and amending of laws, their legal status would have remained what it is?'[14] It was a stance which yoked together their more abstract notions of justice and of equality with practical considerations. Frances Power Cobbe described her own awakening.

It was only after I had laboured sometime with . . . Mary Carpenter [the Bristol philanthropist] . . . and learned to feel intense interest in the legislation which might possibly mitigate the evils of crime and pauperism, that I seriously asked myself *why* I should not seek for political representation as the direct and natural means of aiding every reform I had at heart.[15]

Feminists of all political creeds were unhappy with the performances of successive governments, not merely in direct relation to women's questions but in their attitudes to a host of social and economic problems. Their analysis of those inadequacies rested on the unbalanced nature of representation which denied a voice to outsiders – women and the propertyless poor. The moral argument that women's representation would force parliamentary consideration of matters hitherto neglected was as common a rationale as the broader moral reasoning based on a simple notion of equal justice. Not only was an unrepresentative government 'despotic',[16] but it would inevitably ignore the problems of the unrepresented.

Why should women have freedom? . . . because there is a great deal of moral power amongst them, a great deal of intelligence, a great deal of public spirit which they ought to be called upon to exercise for the good of our common country, for the good of mankind.[17]

Independence and self-development also featured in their arguments. Political participation would release women's potential to the full.

The political background of anti-slavery in which many of these women had grown up was obvious in their choice of language and ideas. Mary Ashton Dilke spoke of their legal minority as tantamount to 'tyranny' while the Women's Emancipation Union castigated the 'slavery of sex'.[18] The echoes of the earlier anti-slavery agitation of the 1830s and 1840s was a deliberate challenge to parliamentary reformers who had been active in the agitation but who seemed reluctant in this context closer to home. The feminist understanding of the advantages of freedom from slavery followed a similar reasoning to that of the earlier protests, that slavery entrenched dependency. 'When will mankind learn, that if they will not allow room for the virtues of independence, they must be content with the vices of dependence?'[19]

In December 1874 an article signed simply B.T. and entitled 'Latest Intelligence from the Planet Venus' appeared in one of the well-known and widely-read periodicals of the day, *Fraser's Magazine*. Claiming that telescopic communication had been recently established between Earth and Venus, the piece went on to describe the remarkable system of government pertaining on Venus where, 'though the present sovereign happens to be a king, all political business, electoral and parliamentary, is allotted to the women'.[20] The article proceeds to describe solemnly the horror induced in parliamentarians by a recent suggestion to extend the suffrage to men.

The notion of admitting young cornets, cricketers and fops . . . to a share in the legislation, the prospect of Parliamentary benches recruited from the racecourse, the hunting-field, and the billiard room, was a picture that proved too much for the gravity of the Commons.[21]

This witty piece by a woman author was a clever demolition of the standard arguments used to dismiss suggestions of a female franchise. Feminists did what they were to do so often in this period; embrace the mainstream view of their position but turn it to full advantage. Thus the force of women's political presence would be a softening and humanizing one. It would 'raise . . . the average quality, as regards conduct, of the existing constituencies', and tend to 'soften our ferocities and purify our whole state'.[22]

The grounds on which women from different feminist organizations demanded the vote did not differ radically. Their arguments tended to cluster around these considerations; their clashes occurred far more commonly over tactics, over means rather than ends. All the suffrage bodies founded during this period used similar methods of persuasion but differed in how extensive a franchise they were prepared to ask for in the first instance.

The earliest organizations were the regional suffrage committees founded in London, Birmingham, Bristol, Edinburgh and Manchester in 1867 and 1868 which together became the National Society for Women's Suffrage (NSWS) in early 1868 (see Figure 1). Two years later, they began publication of the *Women's Suffrage Journal*, edited by Lydia Becker. Becker was the first secretary of the Manchester Women's Suffrage Society which rapidly became an important focal point of activity. The first London committee, like its Manchester counterpart, was of mixed membership, radical men sharing the work with feminist women. The more prominent positions were almost always filled by women, however, with the men as figureheads of respectability. The first secretary of the London committee was Millicent Garrett Fawcett's elder sister, Louisa Smith. Her early death in 1867 saw Caroline Ashurst Biggs replace her. Biggs' family networks were not dissimilar to those of the Garrett family; her aunts were Caroline Stansfeld and Emilie Venturi, both prominent feminists. The Ashurst women apparently even called themselves 'the clan', so conscious were they of their shared stance.[23]

The date of this early activity is significant; though it does not mark the beginning of interest in the suffrage question, it is the point at which organized agitation found a footing. The women's petition of 1866 organized by Barbara Bodichon and her Langham

Figure 1   Women's suffrage societies 1850–1900

1865   'Kensington' Committee London, to
                  gather signatures for petition

1866   Women's Suffrage Provisional Committee, London

1867   Manchester London Edinburgh
                  Society for Women's Suffrage

1868   Bristol Birmingham
                  Society for Women's Suffrage

              National Society for Women's Suffrage

1872   Central Committee, National Society for Women's Suffrage

              London National Society for Women's Suffrage

1877   Central Committee, National Society for Women's Suffrage

1888   National Central Society for   Central Committee National
              Women's Suffrage   Society for Women's Suffrage

1892   National Union of Women's Suffrage Societies

1889   Women's Franchise League

1892   Women's Emancipation Union

Place associates, and presented to parliament by the newly elected radical Liberal John Stuart Mill, came at a time when the whole question of parliamentary reform had once more been revived. 1867 saw the passing of the second Reform Act which, though it did not dilute the connection between full citizenship and property in any significant way, did extend rights to lesser proprietors and to rental properties. Its complete neglect of women was, of course, the most immediate catalyst for feminist action.

The NSWS, which was the fruit of that sense of outrage over the injustices of the 1867 act, petitioned and pamphleted both influential politicans and potential supporters, concentrating heavily – and for obvious reasons – on winning parliamentary notice. 'They set themselves to their task with untiring energy and statesmanlike methods. They organized petitions, deputations, and meetings without end.'[24] By the 1880s, those meetings had become a carefully planned succession of women's demonstrations held in large halls up and down the country and designed to show the strength of feeling on the issue.

In the early 1870s, the NSWS split into two organizations, one still maintaining a national profile with a London-based central committee and the other a smaller London-only organization. They merged again in 1877 as the Central Committee of the NSWS. The break had its origins in a clamour from parliamentary supporters for a shift of focus to Westminster and thus to a standing committee in London. The parting of the two factions would perhaps not have occurred had the contentious feminist involvement in the fight for repeal of the Contagious Diseases Acts not also occurred at this time. Some women, among them Millicent Fawcett, though they favoured the stand taken by their feminist colleagues on the prostitution issue, none the less wished to distance their 'respectable' cause from one with dangerously *risqué* overtones. The new national organization still maintained on its executive Contagious Diseases Acts repeal activists such as Ursula Bright and sisters Caroline Stansfeld and Emilie Venturi. The London bias which these changes implied did not, however, represent a take-over by London-based feminists. The committee's base in London derived only from its need to be close to parliament; the presence of Manchester women Bright and Venturi as well as one of the Edinburgh McLaren women on the central committee is significant. And it is clear that the concentration on parliamentary affairs at no time diminished the importance or strength of provincial activity. In 1881 Laura McLaren wrote to Lydia Becker in Manchester offering her the secretaryship of the London Central Committee.

It appears to us that there is a waste of force in having two centres of political action and although the energy of Manchester is powerfully felt in the country, still, as all parliamentary business must be transacted in London, it is here we need the powerful head to act promptly.[25]

One further schism marred the suffrage cause before the century was over. In 1888, the umbrella organization debated the proposal to open its doors to the new women's sections of the political parties who would enter the feminist organization with the same power and authority as the suffrage societies. The older generation of feminists were unanimously hostile to this suggestion, regardless of their personal political views. Liberals such as Fawcett and Biggs sided with Conservatives Cobbe and Boucherett in forming yet another body – a new Central Committee of the NSWS. Both Garretts – Millicent and her cousin Rhoda – Becker, the Davenport Hill sisters Florence and Rosamond, veteran educationalist Lady Goldsmid, Boucherett, Blackburn and Biggs were all on the executive committee of the breakaway organization. They represented only a minority opinion however; the larger body became the National Central Society for Women's Suffrage, peopled by equally prominent women such as Jane Cobden, Mary Ashton Dilke, Emily Sturge and Frances Buss. The resignations of so many influential and experienced women was none the less undoubtedly a blow. The final reconstitution of the various wings under the banner of the National Union of Women's Suffrage Societies in 1897 was something of a triumph for these renegades; not only was its leadership dominated by them, but the rules of the new organization determined its distance from political affiliation.

There were, in addition to these fractious suffrage organizations, two other important societies active in this work, and sometimes exhibiting an overlapping membership. Elizabeth Wolstenholme Elmy, who had been a prominent figure in both Married Women's Property and Contagious Diseases Acts agitation was one of the founders of the Women's Franchise League (WFL) in 1889. On leaving the WFL, she went on to found the Women's Emancipation Union (WEU) in 1892. Elmy had been involved in suffrage campaigning from its earliest days, collecting signatures for the petition presented in the Commons by Mill in 1866 and as a member of the Manchester NSWS. Her radicalism, added to her unusual private life, had not rendered her popular among the more conservative elements within feminism. Her pre-marital pregnancy had caused consternation and she married only at the urgent bidding of her feminist associates. Sylvia Pankhurst describes her as 'a tiny Jenny-wren of a woman, with bright bird-like eyes, and a little face, child-like in its merriment and its pathos'.[27] She was, none the less, a woman of strong opinion. With some exceptions, the women she gathered round her in her new organizations were more radical in their approach than the NSWS feminists and often active in the various forms of local government open to women. Alice Scatcherd, Agnes Sunley, Florence Fenwick Miller (with whom she later fell out, just as she had done with Ursula Bright), and Harriet McIlquham as well as the Pankhursts, husband and wife, and Clementia Taylor – whom Elmy called 'the grandmother – the doyenne of the Women's Suffrage movement in England'[28] – were her close associates.

Her disagreement with the major suffrage societies, and her reason for founding these new organizations, was the willingness of the older societies to accept a partial measure of franchise. Many women believed that the extension of the franchise to single and widowed women who were property owners or rate-payers in their own right was an acceptable compromise which was less likely to upset the prejudices of the law-makers. The disagreement which surfaced most forcefully in the 1890s when bills of this kind gained a parliamentary footing had, in fact, been foreshadowed in the very earliest days of the movement. Emily Davies mused on the expediency of adopting limited aims at the time of the 1866 parliamentary petition.

Do you think it better . . . in future, to limit our demand definitely to unmarried women and widows? The limitation seems to strengthen our position so much with most people, that one feels tempted to adopt it, if it could be done honestly and without embarrassing future action.[29]

A certain expediency and pragmatism seemed to the women necessary elements of their campaigning, though they led on occasion to some curiously contradictory actions. At the same time as the option of a limited franchise which would prejudice the political standing of the married woman was under consideration, the movement still recognized and wanted to utilize the *cachet* lent them by their prominent married activists. It was Helen Taylor, who was *not* a proponent of the partial option, who none the less wrote to Millicent Fawcett in 1868:

We find, much to our regret that Mrs [Clementia] Taylor intends to send in her resignation of the Secretaryship of the Women's Suffrage Society. I have tried to persuade her to allow her name to remain as at present, Miss Biggs doing the work as assistant secretary, but this she calls a *shame*, and wishes Miss Biggs to be the nominal secretary in her place.

I have urged upon her all such objections as I could – saying that a *Mrs* is better than a *Miss*.[30]

By the 1880s, with the other changes that had affected women – the granting of the municipal franchise to single women and widows, the Married Women's Property Acts – it was an issue which cleaved the movement in two. Millicent Fawcett and Lydia Becker (the former married, though widowed in 1884, and the latter unmarried) continued to believe in the expediency of a limited measure, a stand which brought much criticism from other quarters. '[It would] do far more harm to women collectively, than could be at all to my mind compensated for by the trivial advantages gained by the political rights granted by it to a limited class of women'.[31]

It was to counter this trend among suffragist women that Elizabeth Wolstenholme Elmy founded the WFL and strenuously pointed out the gains which married women had made in the movement's lifetime and the potential they would be discarding by promoting what she called a Spinster and Widow bill. The first stated object of the WFL was, 'To extend to women, whether unmarried, married, or widowed, the right to vote at Parliamentary, Municipal, Local and other elections on the same conditions which qualify men'.[32] The League was not questioning the propertied definition of citizenship which brought about the entitlement to vote, but in the wake of the married woman's newly-won rights to separate ownership of property (see Chapter 6), felt that her exclusion from the franchise would amount to little more than an act 'to propitiate our legislative gods by a sacrifice'.[33]

Elmy had taken with her into the WFL a number of women prominent at an early stage in the campaign's history, notably Ursula Bright, Josephine Butler, Emilie Venturi and Clementia

Taylor. They were all married women whose husbands, for the most part, also joined the WFL. Clementia Taylor had resigned from the Executive Committee of the Central NSWS in late 1884 over its sanctioning of a Spinster and Widow bill, and it is interesting to find Ursula Bright congratulating Millicent Fawcett's husband, Henry, on his stand on this issue in the same year, and shortly before his death. After all, Millicent consistently championed a partial measure of franchise as politically expedient.

Thank you *most heartily* for supporting the claim of qualified married women to the Suffrage. . . . We cannot exclude them without making our selves and our cause ridiculous . . . how sadly we have been weakened by the timidity of our friends both in and out of Parliament.[34]

The problem was complicated by the link between the two issues of property qualification and marital status. Few married women, even after the changes in the laws governing this area, could have claimed the vote and in effect, their political participation would thus imply a universal adult franchise. As Mary Ashton Dilke argued,

Men have not got universal suffrage, and it would of course be quite impossible to ask for women what men have not yet got. . . . The most logical work to be done seems, therefore, to be, to place women who are qualified as the law now stands, on an equality with men, in the hope that when the day of universal suffrage arrives . . . the experiment having proved a successful one, they will be ready to extend the right to all alike.[35]

In the early twentieth century, socialist and liberal women were to clash over the conflicting claims of universal manhood suffrage or propertied women's suffrage as the more urgent cause. In the nineteenth century, however, any visions of a democratic franchise were visions of the future and in no sense of immediate concern. Brian Harrison's assessment that the call for female suffrage needed to yoke itself to the respectability offered by property limitations is largely correct.[36] This was an issue which embroiled them in the mechanics of governing politics where their voice was, as they so often pointed out, an unrecognized one. Their activity was dependent upon parliamentary attention for they were, after all, struggling precisely for representation on or membership of that body. 'We are working for the parliamentary vote, because we feel that must be the bulwark behind which we intrench every other privilege and every other right that we obtain.'[37] The failure of the women's movement to contest the lack of democracy in Britain's politics does suggest, as many commentators have noted, that it was a campaign conducted within a narrow class framework. There was little involvement of working-class women in the clamour for the vote before the turn of the century; even after the passing in 1884 and 1885 of the two acts which together made up the third chapter of parliamentary reform in the nineteenth century, many poorer men were still left voteless. In the nineteenth century, the suffrage campaign was largely composed, as Sandra Stanley Holton has shown, of 'the parliamentary lobbying activities of an élite group of middle-class women'.[38] And yet, at the same time, they were not unaware of class issues and saw their feminist principles as a way of winning a voice as much for working-class women as for themselves. 'The inequality of the sexes in privilege and power, was a great cause of the dreadful hardships which women, especially in the lower classes, had to suffer.'[39]

In a society which did not yet profess democracy and where socialism's effects were still largely confined to the margins, women from secure backgrounds, who were fighting for a right which centrally defined respectability and responsibility, were unlikely to find tactical success in stepping so far from present conditions. Many historians have seen this lack of radicalism as evidence of the pervasive liberalism of the nineteenth-century women's movement, both in its accent on the equality of individuals and in the high proportion of feminists whose own political allegiance leaned in this direction. It is certainly true that most, but by no means all, of their parliamentary contacts were with sympathetic Liberals, but few feminists adhered as closely to liberal doctrines as has been so often suggested. The general consensus that feminist organizations should avoid party affiliation was an important principle; rather than making them apolitical, it rather articulated their chosen distance from dominant politics. 'We would urge women to disregard the ordinary political parties, and to vote for the man who favours justice to women, be his political creed, in other respects, what it may.'[40] In effect, many women skirted the problem by separating out their different political persona. They might indeed belong to one of the women's auxiliaries of the main parliamentary parties but saw this as being a separate affiliation to their feminist involvement. Women who belonged only to the auxiliary bodies had little connection with feminist organizations and accepted more fully their own limited role within the larger male-dominated organizations of which they were part.

On issues such as the suffrage or other measures which necessarily involved legislative change, women had no choice but to seek redress through the obvious political routes. Even where they did so, however, their accent was always on the benefits women could offer, on what Sandra Holton has called the 'feminization' of the public sphere.[41] Their values were not, therefore, those of nineteenth-century liberalism, whether this was seen as a theoretical creed or as an expression of a party political manifesto. Indeed, even feminists who called themselves Liberals were sceptical of its value in the feminist context.

I sometimes take up a Liberal paper, one which never has a good word to say for Women's Suffrage, but in it I find week after week, and day after day, articles complaining of the extravagance, the frivolity, and the mischievous matchmaking propensities of women. . . . I wonder the writer does not see it to be the natural fruit of the system he upholds.[42]

We can, to some extent, assess the differences in male and female perceptions of politics in a practical way by examining the impact of women's contributions in the arena of local government. The *Women's Suffrage Journal* called the Municipal Franchise Act of 1869, 'an engine of great power which cannot fail to produce important results in hastening the time when the full measure of justice shall be conceded'.[43] The act both signalled a preliminary relaxation of prejudices and was an important step in itself. It was the first of a number of measures which, over the following thirty years, were to affect women's participation in a whole range of municipal offices. The 1869 act gave unmarried women ratepayers a vote 'in the election of councillors, auditors and assessors'.[44] In 1870, with the passing of the Elementary Education Act, these women became similarly eligible to vote for and stand in elections to the new School Boards. And in 1875, Martha Merrington became the first woman to be elected to a Poor Law Guardianship. It was not until 1894 that the Local Government Act extended these rights to married women, but from 1870 a trickle of qualified women, many of them feminist activists, contested the various elections. The Committee of the Society for Promoting the Return of Women as Poor Law Guardians boasted many familiar feminist names: Caroline Ashurst Biggs, Harriet McIlquham, Frances Buss, Frances Power Cobbe, Agnes Garrett, Amelia Arnold, Clementia Taylor, Elizabeth Blackwell and a host of others. The slow growth in direct female involvement became a rapid rush in the wake of the 1894 act, with its widening of the franchise at last to married women. In 1892, there were some 136 women among the 28,000 Poor Law Guardians in England and Wales. By 1895, women accounted for some 800 or 900 of the total, though a large number of Boards still had no women members at all.[45] By the close of the century, there were around 1000 women Poor Law Guardians, more than 200 women members of School Boards and about 200 women parish councillors.[46] Women formed 13.7 per cent of the electorate.[47] It was an impressive showing in so short a period of time, more particularly since legislation could do little to counter the prejudices they continued to endure.

The two acts of 1869 and 1894 had not given women access to all local government, and in both the 1880s and the 1890s setbacks were encountered. The London County Council Act of 1888 saw three women candidates put up for election, all of them active feminists. Emma Cons, a suffrage activist best known as the founder of the South London People's Palace (later to become the Old Vic theatre), Miss Cobden, a suffrage activist from the well-known Radical Cobden family and Lady Sandhurst. Lady Sandhurst's success was short-lived, for the male candidate whom she had defeated took legal action against her candidacy on the grounds that her sex made her ineligible. His success in the Court of Appeal prompted the founding of a committee to secure the return of women to the London County Council, a committee which widened its remit in time as the Women's Local Government Society. The success of their adversaries was further entrenched by the London Government Act of 1899 which replaced the older administrative unit of the vestry with new metropolitan boroughs. Women had previously sat on vestries but under the new act could only vote and not run for election on to the new administration. There may well be some significance in the women's defeats being exclusive to London politics; just as the 1870s had seen a concentration on Westminster dominating the parliamentary suffrage movement, so do these defeats perhaps signal the peculiar importance of metropolitan politics and the need, therefore, to exclude women and direct them into the more minor areas. Female involvement in many levels of local politics might be interpreted as an obvious extension of philanthropic and improving work, frequently revealing the workings of class domination. The establishment of School Boards to supervise state schooling procedures and of Poor Law Boards concerned with the relief (and often the incarceration) of the destitute, were clearly areas in which, before government intervention on a significant scale, many middle-class women had found scope for quasi-public charitable work.

The work of local governing bodies is in the nature of collective house-keeping. Children and education, health and sanitation, the provision of food and medicine, the care and control of the sick, have always been held to be within the province of the woman.[48]

We should be careful, however, not to allow this accent on the domestic to obscure the significance of the public political context in which they were now required to act. The elective nature of these bodies meant that women fielded as candidates would have a high public profile, a high degree of accountability if successful and, of course, be required to work in mixed committees. The workload was heavy, involving frequent meetings and inspections and thus a major commitment of time which, property qualifications aside, would exclude working women. It is interesting in this context to note the large number of married women who did make time for local political action in this way. The stand taken by women on a range of issues – from corporal punishment in schools, to sewerage and housing – was generally less allied to political factions and more concerned with improving social conditions. Many of them campaigned on a progressive ticket and were active in ameliorating social problems. Amie Hicks' platform for a School Board election in 1885 concentrated on education which, as well as including 'one good free meal a day', was to be free, compulsory, secular and industrial.[49] Thomas Gautrey remembered that in his day, 'most of the women members of the Board opposed the use of the cane' on boys.[50] In her opposition to corporal punishment, Helen Taylor, a member of the London School Board in the 1880s, used an interesting rationale that caning was the first step to marital violence. 'A boy who is flogged by his teacher grows up in the belief that he has the right to beat his wife . . . where corporal punishment is forbidden the wives have better protection in after life'.[51]

Laying the foundation stone of the Manchester School Board's fifth school in 1877, Lydia Becker's accompanying speech was uncompromising in its statement of the feminist position. 'She said she did not know why cooking was considered an exclusive subject for girls. If she had her own way every boy in Manchester would be taught to mend his own socks and cook his own chops.'[52] Such critical outspokenness was not confined to women as well-established as Becker, though it was clear that the small numbers of women on such committees could make articulacy a problem. When Rosamond Davenport Hill, whose involvement in School Board politics spanned almost twenty years, was reprimanded for her silence, 'she retorted that it was the first time she had heard a woman blamed for holding her tongue'.[53] One of her women colleagues, Honnor Morten, was even more plain-speaking. 'The silent, hard, conscientious committee work done by women, as opposed to the blatant mouthing of the men on board days is most noticeable on large bodies.'[54] Helen Taylor, according to Francis Soutter, was dedicated to 'a resolute obliteration of the ordinary party political bonds'.[55] Yet it is Elizabeth Sturge's recollection that 'we were all at that time tarred with the brush of the Militants'.[56] Elizabeth Wolstenholme Elmy's close friend, Harriet McIlquham, active in Tewksbury local politics, had strong connections both with Elmy's radical suffrage wing and with the Gloucestershire Conservatives. Their stand, in general, was one of pragmatic humanitarianism and a strong concern for women, rather than an involvement in the intricacies of the party political machine.

Women were prepared to cross the political floor at both a local and a national level, not only in their general and justified disregard for the work of the mainstream political parties but also in stepping from the private to the public sphere. Many were prepared to make overt public stands to enhance their claims, despite the hostility this would inevitably attract. When in 1885 Helen Taylor stood as a parliamentary candidate for North Camberwell in order to force the returning officer to reject her nomination on grounds of sexual disqualification, she had behind her a considerable history of similar actions. The 1867 Reform Act had sparked off a number of claims – some successful – from women for registration as voters. One famous case is that of Lily

Maxwell, whose name had been placed accidentally on the register and who cast her parliamentary vote in Manchester in November 1867. The executive committee of the local NSWS surmised from her success that, 'it may therefore be assumed that the legal incapacity of a woman, if it exists at all, is incapacity to be registered as a voter and not incapacity to record her vote when registered'.[57] A year later Lady Scarisbrick and twenty-seven of her women tenant farmers were similarly successful; the revising barristers who scrutinized the electoral registers did not challenge their registration.[58]

Though Manchester appears to have been the centre of such activity, Clementia Taylor and Caroline Ashurst Biggs, as secretaries of the London NSWS, were busily writing to women whose property qualifications would have granted them the right to vote.

We strongly urge you . . . to record your Vote at the coming Elections. The importance of doing so cannot be overestimated. You stand in the position of champions and representatives of thousands of women, whose claims to be placed on the Register have been ignored or denied. Should you fail to vindicate those claims, it will appear that the women of England are indifferent to their political rights. By recording your votes, you will confer a lasting obligation upon many of your countrywomen.[59]

In the *Chorlton v. Lings* case of 1868, the Court of Common Pleas decided against the women who had claimed their right to vote. From then on, the question of the parliamentary franchise was patiently fought through the trying channels of committees, petitions, deputations and demonstrations.

The changing fortunes of the movement over this period has led many writers to compartmentalize the suffrage fight into a number of phases.

I have often thought that the Suffrage Movement passed through three periods. The earliest I have no recollection of, but the period from 1868 to '80 . . . was distinctly recognised and supported, but it was always shoved into a siding to let the express trains go by, and even the slowest train was an express to those who wished the matter shelved.[60]

Lady Balfour's assessment is an astute one in recognizing that other people's priorities were often the relevant factor in determining, at the least, the attention given to the cause in parliament. Brian Harrison uses a convincing argument when he says that the

1867 Reform Act and the 1872 Secret Ballot Act together set back the cause first, by relegating further electoral reform to a distant date, and then, by ensuring that male voters were no longer *openly* responsible to women at election time.[61] After the initial successes of the years 1866–71, however, Harrison sees the remainder of the century as a period of decline.[62] It is difficult to see the chronological distinction in practice. Few real gains in parliamentary terms were made in either 'phase' but there were very few years in which private members' bills on the issue were not tabled; only in 1880 and 1898 was the House spared discussion of the women's suffrage issue. The NSWS's own assessment of the phases of the movement seems, in this light, more accurate. They dubbed 1867–72 a time of 'general reconnoitring', 1872–86 that of 'concentrated effort' and the period from 1886 on, one of 'diffused activity'.[63]

'Nothing but our own steady and simultaneous labour can really elevate our sex', wrote Frances Power Cobbe in 1881.[64] In the suffrage agitation, as in all the other protests to which feminists devoted attention in this period, it was dogged determination and a powerful belief in the face of hostility and diversion which won them, albeit slowly, their successes. Though it was not until 1928 that women won the parliamentary vote on the same footing as men, feminist efforts had kept the issue alive despite indifference and organized opposition.

It is to make the life of a woman of the higher and lower classes more complete, less dependant [sic], less animal and selfish and more noble and spiritual; in fact, to make her a citizen and give her the chance of leading an honest and happy life.[65]

Thus wrote Kate Amberley to a male friend in 1869. And if we are now aware of the constrictions and limitations of those demands, we should remember the enormity of the feminist struggle at this time.

Ultimately it was the condition of women's lives – specifically their dependence on marriage and the sexual division of labor – that determined the shape of nineteenth-century suffragism. We should understand the inability of nineteenth-century feminists to develop solutions adequate to the oppression of women less as a failure of their political imagination or boldness than as a reflection of the state of historical development of capitalism and of male supremacy.[66]

Notes and references

1 *Women and Work* **25** (21 November 1874), p. 4.
2 British Library, Additional Manuscript. 47451, f. 33. Elizabeth Wolstenholme Elmy to Harriet McIlquham, 11 December 1896.
3 Elizabeth Sturge, *Reminiscences of my life* (privately printed, 1928), p. 63
4 Millicent Garrett Fawcett, *What I Remember* (London, 1924), p. 121.
5 Mary Ashton Dilke, *Women's Suffrage* (London, 1885), p. 55.
6 Barbara Caine, 'John Stuart Mill and the English Women's Movement', *Historical Studies* **18** (April 1978), 70, pp. 52–67.
7 Girton College, Cambridge, Emily Davies Papers, Family Chronicle, f. 533. Emily Davies to Anna Richardson, 18 July 1867.
8 Fawcett Library, London, Autograph Letter Collection: Women's Suffrage, 1851–94. Millicent Fawcett to Edmund Garrett, 21 February 1885.
9 Millicent Garrett Fawcett, 'The Women's Suffrage Movement', in Theodore Stanton (ed.), *The Woman Question in Europe. A Series of Original Essays* (London, 1884), pp. 1–29, (p. 5).
10 Millicent Garrett Fawcett, *Women's Suffrage. [A] Speech delivered in the Town Hall, Birmingham, 6 December 1872*, p. 1.
11 Barbara L. S. Bodichon, *Reasons for the Enfranchisement of Women* (London, 1866), p. 2.
12 Frances Power Cobbe, Introduction to Theodore Stanton (ed.), *The Woman Question in Europe*, p. xvi.
13 Lydia Becker, 'Female Suffrage', *Contemporary Review* (March 1867), pp. 307–16 (pp. 308–9).
14 Millicent Garrett Fawcett, 'Why Women Require the Franchise', in Henry and Millicent Garrett Fawcett, *Essays and Lectures on Social and Political Subjects* (London, 1872), pp. 262–91 (p. 271).
15 Frances Power Cobbe, *The Duties of Women. A Course of Lectures* (London, 1881), p. ii.
16 *Women's Suffrage Journal* **I** (2 May 1870), 3, p. 8.
17 Florence Fenwick Miller, *On the Programme of the Women's Franchise League* (n.d. ?1890), pp. 2–3.
18 Dilke, *Women's Suffrage*, p. 52; *The Women's Emancipation Union. Its Origin and Its Work* (Manchester, 1892), p. 9.
19 E. M. Sturge, *Women's Suffrage. [A] Speech delivered in the Town Hall, Birmingham, 6 December 1872*, p. 5.
20 B.T. [Bertha Thomas], 'Latest Intelligence from the Planet Venus', *Fraser's Magazine* 90 o.s., 10 n.s. (December 1874), pp. 763–6, (p. 763).
21 B.T., 'Latest Intelligence', p. 763.

22 Millicent Garrett Fawcett, *Home and Politics. An Address Delivered at Toynbee Hall and Elsewhere* (London, n.d., ?1894), p. 6; 'Sixteen Reasons for Women's Suffrage', *Women's Suffrage Journal* **II** (2 January 1871), p. 1.

23 Diana Mary Chase Worzala, 'The Langham Place Circle: The Beginnings of the Organized Women's Movement in England, 1854–70', Unpublished PhD thesis, University of Wisconsin-Madison, 1982, p. 375.

24 S. J. Tanner, *How the Women's Suffrage Movement Began in Bristol Fifty Years Ago* (Bristol, 1918), p. 10.

25 Manchester Central Reference Library, Suffrage Collection, M50/1/2. f. 38. Laura McLaren to Lydia Becker, 17 February 1881.

26 Ellis Ethelmer [Benjamin Elmy], 'A Woman Emancipator. A Biographical Sketch'. *Westminster Review* **145** (April 1896), pp. 424–8.

27 E. Sylvia Pankhurst, *The Suffragette Movement. An Intimate Account of Persons and Ideals* (London, 1931), p. 31.

28 British Library, Add. MS. 47449, f. 42. E. W. Elmy to H. McIlquham, 12 July 1889.

29 Quoted in A. P. W. Robson, 'The Founding of the National Society for Women's Suffrage 1866–67', *Canadian Journal of History* **VIII** (March, 1973) I, pp. 1–22 (p. 10). Emily Davies to Helen Taylor, 18 July 1866. MS letter from the London School of Economics, Mill-Taylor Collection XIII, II.

30 Fawcett Library, Autograph Letter Collection: I. Women's Suffrage 1851–94. Helen Taylor to Millicent Garrett Fawcett, 31 October 1868.

31 British Library Add. MS. 47449, f. 40. Elizabeth Wolstenholme Elmy to Alice Cliff Scatcherd, 12 July 1889.

32 Manchester Reference Library, Suffrage Collection, M50/2/32/1. *Women's Franchise League*, 1889.

33 *Women's Franchise League. Report of Proceedings at the Inaugural Meeting. London, 25 July 1889*, p. 4.

34 Fawcett Library, Autograph Letter Collection. I. Bright to Fawcett, 8 February 1884.

35 Mary Ashton Dilke, *Women's Suffrage*, p. 88.

36 Brian Harrison, 'Women's Suffrage at Westminster 1866–1928', in Michael Bentley and John Stevenson (eds), *High and Low Politics in Modern Britain. Ten Studies* (Oxford, 1983), pp. 80–122 (p. 97).

37 May Wright Sewall (ed.), *The World's Congress of Representative Women* (Chicago/New York, 1894), Speech of Florence Fenwick Miller, p. 21.

38 Sandra Holton, 'Feminism and Democracy: The Women's Suffrage

Movement in Britain, with particular reference to the National Union of Women's Suffrage Societies 1897–1918'. Unpublished PhD thesis, University of Stirling, 1980, p. 386. This thesis was published as a book, under the title *Feminism and Democracy* in late 1986.

39 *The Autobiography of Mary Smith, Schoolmistress and Nonconformist. A Fragment of Life* (London, 1892) p. 257.

40 *Women's Suffrage Journal*, I (1 Oct. 1870) 8, p. 78.

41 Holton, *Feminism and Democracy*, p. x.

42 Sturge, *Women's Suffrage*, p. 5.

43 *Women's Suffrage Journal*, I (I Oct. 1870) 8, p. 77.

44 32 & 33 Vic., c. 55.

45 David Rubinstein, *Before the Suffragettes. Women's Emancipation in the 1890s* (Sussex, 1986), pp. 167–9.

46 F. K. Prochaska, *Women and Philanthrophy in Nineteenth Century England* (Oxford, 1980), p. 226.

47 Rubinstein, *Before the Suffragettes*, p. 165.

48 Ethel Snowden, *The Feminist Movement* (1911), p. 125.

49 *A Life's Work. Right Honourable Margaret Bondfield* (London, 1949), p. 35.

50 Thomas Gautrey, *'Lux Mihi Laus': School Board Memories* (London, n.d., 1937), p. 116.

51 Gautrey, *'Lux Mihi Laus'*, p. 116.

52 Fawcett Library. Becker Collection. LEB/1. Newspaper Cuttings: *The Chronicle*, n.d.

53 Gautrey, *'Lux Mihi Laus'*, p. 56.

54 Quoted in Rubinstein, *Before the Suffragettes*, p. 170.

55 Francis William Soutter, *Recollections of A Labour Pioneer*, (London, 1923), p. 86.

56 Sturge, *Reminiscences of my life*, p. 64.

57 *Second Annual Report of the Executive Committee of the Manchester National Society for Women's Suffrage* (Manchester, 1869) p. 5.

58 Millicent Garrett Fawcett, 'The Women's Suffrage Movement', p. 11.

59 Manchester Reference Library, Suffrage Collection, M/50/1/9/1, Circular letter. 6 November 1868.

60 Lady Frances Balfour, *Ne Obliviscaris. Dinna Forget*, 2 vols (London, 1930) II. 136.

61 Harrison, 'Women's Suffrage at Westminster', p. 80.

62 Harrison, 'Women's Suffrage', p. 87.

63 *The National Society for Women's Suffrage. The Work of the Central Committee. A Sketch* (London, 1893), p. 3.

64 Frances Power Cobbe, *The Duties of Women* (1881), p. vi.

65 Bertrand and Patricia Russell (eds.), *The Amberley Papers. The Letters and Diaries of Lord and Lady Amberley*, 2 vols (London, 1937), II. pp. 299–300. Kate Amberley to Henry Crompton, 3 January 1869.

66 Ellen DuBois, 'The Nineteenth Century Woman Suffrage Movement and the Analysis of Women's Oppression', in Zillah R. Eisenstein (ed.), *Capitalist Patriarchy and the Case for Socialist Feminism* (New York, 1979), pp. 137–50 (p. 149).

Chronology

1851 Publication of *Westminster Review* article by Harriet Taylor and John Stuart Mill.

1855 Publication of *Women and the Electoral Franchise* by Justitia.

1865 Committee for Women's Suffrage formed; the 'Kensington' committee.

1866 Women's suffrage petition presented to Parliament by John Stuart Mill.
Women's Suffrage Provisional Committee formed.

1867 Lily Maxwell case.
National Society for obtaining Political Rights for Women founded in London.
Manchester Women's Suffrage Society founded.

1868 Women's Suffrage societies founded in Birmingham, Bristol and Edinburgh.
National Society for Women's Suffrage founded.
Chorlton v. Lings case.

1869 Municipal Franchise Act passed.

1870 School Board elections begun with women candidates eligible.
Women's Suffrage Journal began publication.

1871 London National Society for Women's Suffrage founded.

1872 Central Committee of National Society for Women's Suffrage established in London.

1875 First woman Poor Law Guardian elected.

1877 New Central Committee of National Society for Women's Suffrage formed.

1881 Women granted franchise, Isle of Man.

1888 Central National Committee of Women's Suffrage established.
Central Committee of National Society for Women's Suffrage splits off.

First women elected to London County Council.

Committee to secure the return of women to county councils established.

1889 Women's Franchise League founded.

1892 Women's Emancipation Union founded.

1894 Women permitted candidacy for Parish and District Councils. Local Government Act passed.

1897 National Union of Women's Suffrage Societies established.

4 Employment and the professions: middle-class women and work

Introduction

It seems to me that there are only two great questions at present really before the public. These are the labour question and the women's question. And when we come to consider, these questions really are united; for it is largely on the economic condition of woman that her freedom in the future will depend.[1]

As Harriet McIlquham hints in her address to the Women's Franchise League, the employment of women in Victorian England was hindered by two factors. On the one hand, women shared with male workers the insecurities of employment brought about by the fluctuations so characteristic of the Victorian economy and, on the other, they battled alone against the voice of propriety which sought to define them within an exclusively domestic environment. When looking at women's work in this period and at the varied campaigns connected with it – for better training, more varied openings, improved conditions or wage parity – we must thus look not only at the contemporary feminist readings of the problems but also, more broadly, at the vagaries of the Victorian economy, and the suffering brought in its wake.

For women, the issue of employment was connected with their claims for independence, for a share in the public domain, and with the demand for an identity defined by self-respect. This was the case for middle-class women, at least, and one that early feminists promoted. For working-class women, as well as an increasing proportion of penniless middle-class women, employment was less a source of identity than of subsistence. As Patricia Branca has maintained, 'working-class women as a group never chose to make employment a primary means of identification in their lives'.[2] While campaigns in the 1850s and 1860s concentrated on the expansion of genteel employments suitable for well-

connected women, the later decades of the century saw concerted
efforts towards the unionizing of women workers and hence an
emphasis on broader related issues such as working conditions,
legislative restrictions on female employment and wage levels.
Although there were activists who involved themselves in both
sets of campaigns, the two wings of the women's employment
movement remained largely separate. The characteristic which
separated their interests and tactics most strongly was, therefore,
that of class, a division which served to mark differences in organization, in personnel and in aims. This chapter will deal with the
earlier bourgeois campaigns; Chapter 5 will look at women's trade
unions, the debate around protective legislation and other issues
more commonly associated with working women.

*

One of the most distinctive features of the early campaigns of the
1850s and 1860s concerning this issue was the seemingly unconten-
tious assumption that the problem of finding suitable employment
for women was limited to the single woman. There is little
evidence to suggest that employment campaigners were at all
interested in speculating on the ideal of married middle-class
women's work.[3] The external catalysts for the concern with
middle-class employments were the prophesied rise in the ranks
of women for whom marriage was to prove unattainable, and the
evident and increasing failure of middle-class families to maintain
large retinues of unproductive and unmarried daughters. The very
basis of the Victorian middle-class ideal of the leisured wife and
daughters was netted with internal contradictions; where those
daughters failed to find husbands to replace fathers, they became
unforeseen long-term financial burdens.

It is heartrending to think of the hidden tragedies which these sociological
changes brought in their train, the mute sufferings of the women, who,
unmated and workless, felt themselves of no value or importance to the
world around them. What wonder then that in the end a revolt came,
and women insisted that in the great world of human activities outside
the family they, too, must have place and power.[4]

For such women, the spectre of a double failure loomed large.
The inability to attract a husband marked them out in the circles
of Victorian gentility, while their upbringing and education did

not prepare them in any sense for the world of work. Not only were women looking for paid work hanging, as Maria Grey put it, 'like Mahomet's tomb between the earth of the vulgar and the heaven of gentility',[5] but they were also faced with fierce competition for such meagre openings as were available to them. When the Post Office Savings Bank opened its clerical doors to women applicants, the response was overwhelming. 'We regret, although we are not surprised to learn, that the number of applicants has been so great, that Lord John Manners is obliged to refuse any more nominations'.[6]

The problem which mid-century feminists perceived, therefore, was that ever increasing numbers of women were vying for a largely fixed number of openings within narrowly proscribed fields of activity. Their aims, through the organizations they set in train and through the journals which voiced their views, were to extend women's capabilities and qualifications through education and training, and to combat the prejudices which barred women from many avenues of employment. They were concerned only with 'ladies', with women of breeding whose respectability was crucially at stake in the search for paid employment.

This was not, however, merely a pragmatic response to penury; the feminist contribution to the expansion of female employment opportunities is perhaps more important at the theoretical than at the practical level. The projects they established did succeed in placing women in jobs, but the numbers they aided were inevitably tiny. They did, however, bring a fresh and positive set of attitudes into prominence, based not so much on the threat of poverty as on the dignity and fulfilment which remunerative labour could offer. Their concern with work as a worthy and indeed morally beneficial alternative to the domestic role marks their distance from those who campaigned in the working-class arena; though paid employment was quite clearly an urgent necessity for many middle-class women, the feminists were also concerned with aspects of choice. The young Lydia Becker, later a prominent figure in the suffrage movement, wrote to her aunt: 'employment is what I have long wanted; something to occupy my mind when I could feel that day by day I had done my work and accomplished something'.[7] Mary Smith, the Carlisle schoolmistress, added independence to the qualities that employment encouraged. 'I was determined to fight for my own living, and be a burden to no one'.[8] Frances Power Cobbe, having cast aside the role of unmarried sister in her brother's wealthy household, was delighted when she secured a position writing editorials for a London periodical. '[This was] something for which many prophets and preachers of old would have given a house full of silver and gold. And I was to be *paid* for accepting it!'[9]

The question of payment was, of course, a central issue. The vast unpaid labour force which constituted Victorian philanthropic endeavour was composed principally of women. Their presence was acceptable not only because the offices they fulfilled were regarded as representative of feminine qualities but also because their volunteer status was, in effect, a declaration of respectability and of moral sanctity. When their labours were a source of pecuniary gain rather than of personal sacrifice, the issue became one of respectability. Pioneer doctor Sophia Jex-Blake clashed with her father, a retired lawyer, over precisely this issue. Offered a tutorship in mathematics at Queen's College, her father would only consent to her accepting it if she did so unpaid. Her unsuccessful attempts to alter his opinion reveal the way in which the feminist ethic both echoed the male *status quo* and offered an implicit criticism of its double standard.

You, as a man, did your work and received your payment, and no one thought it any degradation, but a fair exchange. Why should the difference of my sex alter the laws of right and honour? . . . Then there is the honest, and I believe, perfectly justifiable pride of *earning*. Did you not feel this when you received your first salary?[10]

Sophia was not unique in pointing to the contradiction whereby a man's earnings were honest and honourable and a woman's degrading. The early feminist publication, the *Alexandra Magazine* spoke in its first issue of women wage earners as 'these honourable breadwinners'.[11]

And if the tightrope of respectability was a significant handicap given the constraints imposed in polite Victorian society, it was only one of the host of structural problems and personal prejudices encountered by feminist campaigners. Middle-class women shared with their working-class sisters the problem of a heavily circumscribed field of opportunity. The 'governess problem' which so titillated Victorian sensibility from the 1840s encapsulates the difficulties thus imposed. At that juncture, so few occupations were mutually acceptable to society and to the needy woman that governessing rapidly became an overstocked, underpaid and hugely exploited field of labour. 'From first to last they are the victims of gentility.'[12] Feminists pinpointed the absurdity of delivering educational responsibilities into the hands of women unprepared and untrained for the task. In doing so, they challenged the widespread notion of women's natural capacities for child-rearing. And it was this question of training which was to be so prominent a feature of early feminist employment campaigns, a stress which highlights the particular connection with the pragmatic base of educational feminism.

Want of training is the first and greatest drawback to the employment of women. . . . How can we expect habits of consistent industry to succeed a girlhood of negligence or thorough attention to work to follow the frivolous use previously made of her time?[13]

Feminists saw women's unpreparedness for the eventuality of earning their own living as one of their principal targets. Jessie Boucherett, one of the founders of the Society for Promoting the Employment of Women (SPEW), pointed out that women came for assistance to her society only 'when they are utterly without resources, so that they have not the means of paying for instruction nor of maintaining themselves during the period of training'.[14] They were concerned with the ideology which prohibited occupation as well as with the practical tasks of locating potentially fruitful areas of work. At that level, the prejudices and fears they encountered in their efforts mirrored antagonism back on to them; if the act of paid work was to coarsen and de-sex the essentials of femininity, so too would feminist activists suffer. If a loss of respectability and caste were the rewards for wage labour, so they were for feminists as well. Both campaigners and the women they strove to help were trespassers in the public sphere and pilloried for their efforts accordingly. And yet, with the economic changes consonant on industrialization, new employments in a variety of sectors emerged and with them, a feminist determination to see them opened to women. The campaign around the employment of middle-class women in the paid work-force centred on the questions of opportunity and of choice for the single woman, and of course implicit too in that notion was that of her choice of whether or not to marry. Their demands and efforts were couched in the name of justice, a justice in which the working woman and the single woman were no longer ideological outcasts.

It is work we ask, room to work, encouragement to work, an open field with a fair day's wages for a fair day's work; it is injustice we feel, the injustice of men, who arrogate to themselves all profitable employments and professions, however unsuited to the vigorous manhood they boast, and thus, usurping women's work, drive women to the lowest depths of penury and suffering.[15]

The earliest feminist efforts in this area date from the activities of the Langham Place Circle in London in the late 1850s. Their close involvement in the new National Association for the Promotion of Social Science reflects their interest in contemporary social issues, and to some extent their desire to find alternatives to the traditional philanthropic palliatives with which social problems were customarily met. The Langham Place women offered a central metropolitan conduit through which a variety of radical and feminist experiments flowed. Their journal, the *English Woman's Journal*, edited by Bessie Rayner Parkes, was the first of many such feminist periodicals which were to raise this and related issues.

Alongside the journal and reading room set up at Langham Place came the first of the women's employment societies. Founded in 1859, the Society for Promoting the Employment of Women was 'formed for promoting the Training of Women and their employment in industrial pursuits'.[16] The society bore the stamp of respectability with its host of eminent patrons headed by the queen herself. Many of the most prominent activists of the day sat on its committee – Millicent Fawcett, Frances Buss, Jessie Boucherett, Helen Blackburn – and outside London, it was women such as Emily Davies in Gateshead and Jessie Cowen in Nottingham who formed separate branches in their locales. In 1867, 80 per cent of the society's subscribers were women.[17]

The stated aim of the society was twofold; to train women and to find employment for them. To this end, it began by establishing a register of women seeking employment, to whom it hoped to act as a form of labour exchange. In this respect, the enterprise was moderately successful, although the number of applicants far outstripped the work available, as had always been anticipated. Simultaneously the London SPEW established classes in book-keeping, a skill of increasing value in Victorian society and an occupation which, its associations with money aside, was unlikely to attract a label of feminine unsuitability. Also under its auspices began an all-women law-copying office and Emily Faithfull's printing establishment, the Victoria Press, where all the compositors were women. Aware of the educative functions of their project, the society also actively sought out employers who might hire its 'graduates'. The regional branches of the society followed a similar blueprint, adjusted according to the specific circumstances pertaining in their localities.

The work of the society did expand, though modestly, with time; in 1876, an office for tracing engineers' and architects' plans was added to the existing and successful all-women enterprises already in existence. As one of its founders stated, however, 'it is evident that a Society with an income of less than £400 a year can do little towards providing training for the girls of a great metropolis'.[18]

The inevitability of meagre funding was only one of the problems which feminist campaigners faced in this field. In dealing with an issue such as employment, they were in essence taking on a powerful and antagonistic economic lobby which manifested itself in two ways – the power of employers and the power of male trade unions.

It was at one time hoped that glass engraving was to have been a great success for good and elegant work was executed by the girls who were taught at the society's expense, but trades unions made it impossible for them to obtain employment.[19]

Even more powerful was the combination of the two hostile forces of male capital and male labour which banded together to secure the male prerogative.

In 1897, a Miss L. M. Wilkinson was refused entry to classes at London's Central School of Arts and Crafts. The school's co-director blamed her exclusion on objections raised by the trade rather than by his institution.

The lady kept pressing the point that she was being refused because she was a woman . . . that was a matter between the trade and women, but if they could settle the matter favourably, *we* should be very glad to take women.[20]

The luckless Miss Wilkinson could thus not even secure the training with which she might fight for entry into the trade. And the interpretation which the school's director chose to make is an interesting one. Working-class men, principally through their union activities, were made to bear the burden of responsibility for prohibiting the free choice of women, with their employers taking refuge behind the union banner in a manner which, in any other form of industrial dispute, would be highly unlikely.

There were, none the less, avenues of employment where even such formidable combinations as these could not prevent women's incursion. Considering the employment of women as Post Office telegraphists, a commentator noted that,

the wages which will draw men from but an inferior class will draw women from a superior class, and hence they will generally write better than the former and spell more correctly; and that they are less disposed than men to combine for the purpose of extorting higher wages.[21]

To some degree, the premium which societies like the SPEW placed on respectability and gentility dug them ever deeper into the trap of occupational suitability in this way. Faced with the hostility of those who held the purse-strings and the power, their choices were stark. The conclusion is inescapable that women were, more often than not, channelled into jobs regarded as 'inferior' to those held by men, or whereby their acceptance as co-workers automatically downgraded that work. Within the parameters in which they were thus forced to work, women campaigners none the less voiced a distinctively feminist response.

Emily Faithfull's revolutionary printing venture, the Victoria Press, is an interesting example of the way in which these women sought to combine the practical advantages which women could gain from their efforts with their specifically feminist readings of the situation. The Victoria Press, in which all the compositors were women whom Faithfull had herself trained, rapidly became the feminist printing house of the period. As well as producing her own journals – the *Alexandra Magazine* and the *Victoria Magazine* – she printed many of the other feminist periodicals of the day and a host of women's pamphlets and tracts besides. Her venture attracted a predictable flurry of attention, and critics immediately pounced upon her continued employment of men for the really heavy tasks. Emily Faithfull's work practices, however, exhibited an interesting rationale and, moreover, an overt criticism of working conditions in other establishments. At the Victoria Press she was careful to implement humane conditions and reasonable wages and hours for her employees. 'She insisted upon open windows and regular periods of relaxation, and so safeguarded her workwomen from the industrial diseases which were then prevalent among printers.'[22]

The Victoria Press had intimate connections with the SPEW and though both offered women a fresh approach to the problem of finding paid labour, their effects were necessarily restricted. In its first ten years of existence, the society succeeded in finding permanent positions for forty-eight women and temporary openings for a further forty-six. For the most part, their success was in the more obvious areas. Nine nurses, eight wardrobe-keepers and matrons and seven saleswomen are their most prominent successes; ten women found apprenticeships in unspecified 'unusual' trades.[23] The employments in which they placed applicants were largely non-industrial and non-manual, though there were two lace-cleaners and a hairdresser. The class gap between industrial and other employments remained large, and where such women did take up manual employments these tended to be in more sedate areas. The Royal School of Art Needlework, opened in 1872, employed between 100 and 150 needlewomen of genteel background in a trade with the right air of domestic suitability.[24] Similarly, in the manufacturing sector, such women would find work as designers and artists rather than in the production process itself. A society such as the SPEW could not hope, given its size and its scant funds, to do more than point out the implications of this insistence on gentility, and the contradictions it entailed. 'The perception by men of the unfeminine character of any kind of labour, arises and grows very keen only when the labour is remunerative, and carries with it any social privilege or dignity.'[25]

In August 1874 a body entitled the National Union of Working Women (NUWW) was set up, with the help of the WPPL's Emma Paterson in Bristol under the trusteeship of Millicent Fawcett and two male sympathizers. Although the union was to survive the century, it underwent something of a metamorphosis from being, in its earliest years, a body with defined trade union links, to one which, by the late 1890s, had become little more than another philanthropic society. Its initial stated aims had been not only the formation of women's unions and of benefit funds for the contingencies of illness and death, but in addition a monitoring of legislation affecting women's employment. By the 1890s, its committees included members of 'ladies' ' associations for the care of girls, and its constitution had become distinctly less radical. It wished rather 'to promote the social, moral and religious welfare of women in general'.[26] A smattering of feminist activists lent their names or subscribed to the organization – Josephine Butler, Clementia Taylor, Alice Scatcherd in its early years, Lady Balfour, Clara Collet, Louisa Hubbard in the 1890s – but few played any prominent part in determining its policies.

By the end of the century, a few more such organizations had been formed, concerned principally with the plight of middle-class women or composed exclusively of middle-class activists; the Women's Employment Defence Association, an anti-protective legislation watchdog, the Gentlewomen's Employment Club (for women *willing to exert themselves* [their emphasis]) and the Working Ladies' Guild. They could do little more than scratch the surface of the problem. The hundred women placed in jobs by the SPEW and the conferences organized by the NUWW were important but undeniably small-scale steps.

Another important aspect of feminist involvement in employment campaigns was the establishment of feminist periodicals, either devoted principally to this issue or at the least offering a coverage of new trades for women, as well as carrying job advertisements. Edited by Louisa M. Hubbard, *The Year-Book of Women's Work* was first published in 1875. It was aimed, according to its introduction, at the single woman in search of employment and offered a directory of suitable types of labour. In the same year, Hubbard also started her monthly *Woman's Gazette – or news about work*, which changed its name in 1880 to *Work and Leisure*, and was sustained in this latter form until the end of 1893. Emily Faithfull published a similar though weekly journal, *Women and Work*, from 1874. They all carried a variety of articles on topics of interest to women as well as guides and advice in the search for employment, articles on specific trades and, of course, job advertisements.

To help, if possible, those who desire to help themselves, to direct those who wish to tread the path of industry and to encourage the faint-hearted, who have to fight the battle of life against overwhelming odds, is the aim and object which we have set before us.[27]

There were so few ways in which women could find such jobs and so little endorsement in mainstream literature, that these feminist ventures played an important role. They were cheap – Faithfull's *Women and Work* retailed at one penny – encouraging and informative, and introduced women to a whole gamut of related issues. Their positive and often moral position on women's usefulness offered not just comfort but an alternative interpretation to that of the destitute and sad governess who graced the pages of popular literature. Bessie Rayner Parkes' serial 'Letters to Women on Money Earning', in the *Alexandra Magazine* catches exactly this tone of practical righteousness.

Let us therefore, first ask ourselves what earning of money really means, when the idea is peeled to its simplest meaning. It implies the helping to produce something useful or otherwise desirable, in exchange for which people will willingly give money. And if women can render useful service to society, either in direct way of production, or by contributing to art, or literature, or education, they certainly ought to do so. There is nothing in the idea itself either degrading, or which is more to the present purpose, *unfeminine* (December 1864, p. 54).

In a sense, the most potent way in which activist women could extend the cause of women's employment was by themselves moving into new areas of opportunity. Many prominent feminists did just this, taking up employment in government jobs as factory and sanitary inspectors, in the new 'female' professions of nursing and teaching or by fighting for entry into hitherto closed professions such as medicine. Others, such as cousins Agnes and Rhoda Garrett (part of the very active feminist Garrett network) set themselves up in business, and were enormously successful as interior designers, their services being in great demand both within their feminist circles and beyond.

The slow process of attrition whereby women dismantled the barriers to their professional ambitions was fraught with difficulties. The definition of 'the professional' was paradoxically both expanding and narrowing in this period; expanding in that new areas of professional expertise were growing up, other than the three traditional ones of medicine, the law and the clergy, and narrowing in that entry into these areas was more and more restricted by the requirements of training and qualification. It was this latter, of course, which served so often to bar the way to women. The case of Miss Wilkinson at the Central School of Arts and Crafts was not an isolated incident.

One area in which women made successful incursion in the closing years of the century was within the government's factory inspectorate. In 1892, four women had been appointed Assistant Commissioners to the Royal Commission on Labour – May Abraham, Clara Collet, Eliza Orme and Margaret Irwin. The following year, the Home Office appointed Abraham, along with Mary Paterson, to the factory inspectorate, while at the municipal level, the Kensington Vestry in London appointed two women sanitary inspectors, Rose Squire and Lucy Deane. By 1896, five women were employed by the Factory Department of the Home Office as part of the inspectorate, whilst Clara Collet had taken up an appointment at the Board of Trade in 1893. Their success was the culmination of some twenty years of lobbying. Both working-class and middle-class women's organizations had long argued that women inspectors were an important addition to existing arrangements. As well as women's trade unions and similar organizations, the SPEW had also lobbied on this issue. Margaret Bondfield, who was to become a prominent Labour politician in the early twentieth century, recalled the hindrances these early calls for change faced. 'In 1878 Mrs Emma Paterson [founder of the Women's Protective and Provident League: see Chapter 5] brought the question before the Bristol Trades Union Congress, and secured their approval year after year. "You can pass it," said one prominent Trade Unionist, "they'll never get it!" '[28]

In common with other Civil Service appointments, the women candidates for these positions were required to sit the general Civil Service entrance examination. Rose Squire remembered composing an essay on the relative merits of music, painting and sculpture, taking a dictation from a Walter Scott novel and sitting an oral test on the existing Factory Law.[29] This reliance on examination scores raises some interesting points; it assumes, of course, that the applicant is educated to a certain standard and in a particular way, and indeed, the universities of both Oxford and Cambridge trained young men explicitly for the examinations of the Indian Civil Service, if not the home one. Second, the subjects in which candidates were examined bore little relation to the jobs in which they would thereafter be placed, a curious quirk which rather complicates our understanding of professionalism but which, if anything, helped ease women into government service.

Whereas more directly vocational trainings such as those required for the legal and medical professions remained an almost closed book to women throughout the century, the preference expressed by the Civil Service for candidates with a good general education thus aided the entry of women who could not, after all, rely on a network of contacts for their appointment.

These early women appointees were largely, though not wholly, women with a strong educational history and Adelaide Anderson and Clara Collet, at least, were products of the new feminist schools and colleges. Anderson had gone on to Girton College after a secondary education at Queen's College, Harley Street, and Collet had followed her years at Frances Buss's North London Collegiate School with a stunningly successful career at University College London. She was not only the college's first woman fellow, but London University's first woman MA. May Tennant, on the other hand, had received no formal education prior to her appointment.

At the vocational level, Hilda Martindale, appointed in 1901, Rose Squire and Lucy Deane all had some training in hygiene. On leaving Royal Holloway College in 1895, Martindale studied Hygiene and Public Health at Bedford College, whilst Squire and Deane were both appointed London sanitary inspectors in the year they began training as hygiene, nursing and first aid lecturers for the National Health Society. May Abraham's qualifications for the job were peculiar but apt; she had acted as secretary to her aunt, trade union activist Lady Dilke, in the late 1880s and through that connection had become treasurer of the Women's Trade Union League.

Despite their training or experience, however, these early women inspectors were still ill-prepared for the duties which they assumed and many of the tasks they were expected to undertake.

No-one could have have known less about industrial conditions, the intricacies of machinery, factory workers and the Factory Acts . . . on the fifth day I found myself inspecting workshops alone in West London, and in the shortest possible time conducting proceedings, again alone, in the Bow Street Police Court and at the Mansion House, with the flimsiest knowledge of the law I was administering or of Police Court procedure.[30]

Given the nature of Civil Service appointments, the women were certainly no less well qualified than male members of the inspectorate, though their wages were lower. They were, though, subject to many more difficulties, difficulties reflected quite clearly in the choice of language the service employed. *Lady* inspectors were engaged to service the needs of *women* workers, as Helen Jones has pointed out.[31] Rose Squire noted the linguistic history of a similar convention.

We women inspectors were officially known first as female inspectors, then as lady inspectors, and finally as women inspectors. The change in convention perhaps reflects the change that has taken place in women's position in the Civil Service in that period.[32]

Not surprisingly, in the early years of what Adelaide Anderson has called this 'administrative adventure', women's scope was more limited than men's. As well as confining their attention to women's work, even within that sphere there were issues such as the fencing of machinery which were automatically referred to the men.[33] Where the women looked into questions of working conditions and practices, it was the men to whom questions involving technology were directed. Unlike the men, the women were appointed to look after women workers' general interests, whereas the men were assigned to specific trades.[34]

None the less, as Helen Jones argues, the type of work they undertook and their attitude towards it absolved them from accusations of any easy transference from the duties required of middle-class daughters and wives.[35] Unlike women Poor Law Guardians or the early one-off appointment of Jane Senior to a workhouse inspectorship, investigating women's industrial working conditions was a directly and boldly public affair. Their presence and their determination, as well as the general commitment to women's causes which many of them maintained, marks their efforts out as an aspect of feminist campaigning. Many of these women had been involved with feminism prior to their government appointments and generally kept up the work they had begun there. May Tennant and Clara Collet both had connections with Bedford College, Tennant as a council member and Collet as a governor. Adelaide Anderson and Collet had connections with the Women's Co-operative Guild and Tennant, of course, with the Women's Trade Union League. Clara Collet made her feminist mark chiefly through her writings. In 1890 she published *The Economic Position of Educated Working Women* which was followed by numerous other publications in and around the area of women's employment. The title of this early work is interesting; Collet herself fitted the description and after her successes at University College had taught in a Leicester girls' school for some seven years. These early pioneers were fully conscious of their unusual positions. By the close of the century, however, the idea of women in government positions was becoming more acceptable: women – indeed feminist – commissioners had been appointed to the Bryce Commission on Secondary Education; Clara Collet was employed in the Home Office as Correspondent to the Labour Department, in which office she detailed important statistics on the nature and extent of women's labour; and increasing numbers of women occupied positions of similar standing in local authorities, as medical officers and within the various inspectorates.

There were tougher nuts to crack, however, than the prejudices of the Home Office. If the medical profession at least proved malleable in this period, that of the law remained unassailable. It is difficult to assess why this should have been, though it is as well to note that the energies successfully expended on medical qualifications were not turned in this period in any serious way on the legal world. The response of the medical establishment to early women's victories was to seal up the cracks in their armour thus made visible. When Elizabeth Blackwell was triumphantly placed on the British Medical Register in 1859, the profession's response was prompt; no foreign medical qualifications were to be acceptable hereafter. Women had no access to training in Britain and so one avenue to recognition was effectively shut off. This cat and mouse game continued for some years, with the women taking legal action in some instances; but against all odds and with huge support, financial and moral, from the feminist community in general, qualified women doctors began practising in England in the 1870s. The numbers were, of course, tiny; in December 1880 there were twenty-one British-registered medical women though numbers grew rapidly thereafter. By 1894, there were around 170 medical women on the register.[36] 'Their presence will tend in an eminent degree to the preservation of health as distinct from the cure of disease, at any rate as far as women patients are concerned.'[37] Most of them built their reputations and their practices on devoting their skills to the care of women and children patients. Elizabeth Garrett in particular acted as medical adviser to a sizeable portion of the London feminist network and yet, despite her staunch espousal of feminist principles, there was at times a clash between that and the requirements of the profession. It was as a member of the medical establishment that Garrett supported the implementation in the 1860s of the Contagious Diseases Acts; as a feminist we might have expected her to oppose them. We find her asserting in 1870 that legislation imposing the enforced examination and treatment of prostitutes for venereal disease (see Chapter 6), 'is strictly a professional question, upon which the opinion of trustworthy medical witnesses ought to be accepted as final. It is enough if unprofessional persons know what that opinion is'.[38] Thus, though the acquisition of professional status lent women a new autonomy, it also exercised some degree of control by imposing upon them existing and therefore male-defined standards. Meredith Tax similarly noted an ensuing careerism among women trade union organizers as they consolidated their positions as women labour leaders.[39] And yet, as Brian Harrison has pointed out, there was more at stake for these women than simply proving their capacity for professional status. Their feminist activism, even where it was tempered as in the controversy over the Contagious Diseases Acts, signalled the significance of gaining medical expertise as 'a pronounced concern for the privacy of the female person'.[40] Women doctors and women administrators had an immediate identification by sex which might mediate the impersonality of professional behaviour.

In some ways, the problems were more acute for women entering nursing or teaching, precisely because they were the areas which rapidly became associated with, almost defining of, women's professionalization. The care of the sick and of children were, of course, acceptable areas of activity for women; the gap between the 'lady with the lamp' and the real Florence Nightingale pinpoints the dilemma.

Ladies who desire to study and practise medicine are told that it is unfeminine and unladylike, besides being too laborious for their sex, and are urged instead to become nurses. . . . The strains upon the nerves and physical strength, the violence done to delicacy, the necessity of witnessing painful and disgusting sights, are greater in the case of the nurse . . . while many of the offices that have to be performed by her, are in themselves of so repulsive a character to anyone not bred to menial service, that only strong affection or enthusiasm could overcome the disgust attending them; but then, neither high pay nor social position are to be attained by the nurse, while both are claimed by the physician. It has, therefore, been decided that it is highly unfeminine, nay, revolting to every feeling of womanly delicacy, for a woman to be a physician, but most feminine to be a nurse.[41]

The status of midwifery, somewhere between medicine and nursing, offers another interesting case study. Midwives were used far more commonly than doctors to attend births. They were cheaper, female for the most part, more accessible – and often untrained. Their efforts to attain recognition and training frequently met with hostility from the medical establishment for whom such a move spelt a potential loss of revenue. If patients were to opt for the attendance of a midwife over a doctor at their confinement, this women's world would represent definite competition for male doctors.

Nursing was an exclusively female profession in the latter half of the nineteenth century, unlike teaching, where the tendency was for women employees to be concentrated in the lower ranks of the profession. It is difficult to generalize about teaching in a period where schooling was conducted by such a variety of bodies; there was a vast difference, in terms of class, status and earnings, between the highly educated women employed in private fee-paying institutions (see Chapter 2) and the elementary school teachers of the post-1870 state sector.[42] In the state sector, training, where it occurred, was a far more desultory affair, often conducted through the pupil-teacher scheme whereby schools apprenticed their own school-leavers to the job for a lengthy period. There was a statutory inequality in the wages of men and women teachers at all levels of the profession, though comparisons were not all that common given their relative positions within the hierarchy. The class distinction whereby well-trained – which largely meant privately-trained, and often in feminist-inspired institutions – middle-class women were channelled into private girls' schools and the working-class recipients of the state's schemes into elementary schools effectively limited feminist achievement to the private sector. We have seen, in Chapter 2, how the curriculum differed in the new private and public institutions, and this feature of the system rubbed off, of course, on those employed there. Feminist campaigners did not tackle state-directed education, preferring to concentrate their efforts else-where. In consequence, the attractions for feminist teachers lay in the conditions and philosophy of the middle-class schools and not in state elementary schooling. It was also in the private sector that professional organizations providing women with a distinct career identity flourished – such as the London Schoolmistresses' Association.

It was clearly necessary for women to move into areas of professional employment as a means not simply of finding paid labour, but as a statement of purpose and of proof of competence. The value placed upon professional status and the jealousy with which that was guarded underlined its superiority within the hier-archy of the Victorian labour market. In claiming the rights to which men had access, professional employment was one obvious area of attack, though in making that claim, of course, women in some respects relinquished their freedom of criticism. Whereas Emily Faithfull, in a skilled trade such as printing, could improve upon the working conditions generally found in such establish-ments, women entering the professional world – where one of the defining characteristics was the non-manual nature of the work, making it ironically a most suitable female environment – were forced to accept its rules, and often did so uncritically.

. . . for older and for highly educated women – for those to whom the keeping up of a social position has become a moral necessity, and for those who have others dependent upon them – we surely ought to seek some employment which will secure them a fair income and not consign them to simple trades, which, let them be ever so extended over numbers, cannot be parellel to the other professions which gentlemen require, or to the commercial enterprise which they carry on on a large scale.[43]

And as David Rubinstein points out, the handful of women who did succeed in this context often did so at considerable personal expense: 'expensive and arduous years of training, the sacrifice of marriage and, in some cases, of a normal private life'.[44]

For the women caught midway between the higher echelons of the professions and the manual labour in which most of the female work-force of the nation was employed, there were a host of additional problems. Margaret Bondfield remembered 'the bitter-ness of a hopeless search for work', in the London of the mid 1890s.[45]. It was a situation all too familiar; an earlier generation of activists had faced the problem when the employment register of the SPEW overflowed with applicants, most of whom stood to receive little more than tea and sympathy. And not only were women in competition with one another, but in some ways with men as well. A large proportion of the available jobs were sex-specific, more particularly as technological innovation led in the later years of the century to de-skilling. This in turn frequently saw the reclassification of jobs once regarded as a male province as lower paid women's work. As Janet Courtney gloomily noted:

What is the outlook for the bright intelligent girl brought in to do permanently the routine work formerly left to boys just leaving school?. . . .

For a time it works well. The girls show a zeal and a zest which no boy thinks of emulating. But the trouble comes when they grow to be middle-aged women and are still kept at work only fit for beginners.[46]

Women were, willy-nilly, placed in a false competition with men, a competition run on male terms. Women were required to prove their worth, even given the simple facts of their long-term involvement in all manner of trades and skills. As Bulley and Whitley noted, demolishing the grounds of this unequal race: 'Disquisitions as to what women can do, or cannot do, are irrelevant at the present moment, when facilities for training and employment have not been open long enough to test their powers in any direction.'[47]

The conjunction of economics and politics which characterizes the workings of labour and employment made this aspect of feminist campaigning one of the most difficult they were to encounter. Ideological factors combined with hard-nosed economic motives in the contradictory stance which Victorian England took on the employment of women. The careful and controlled assault of the feminist movement on the impact of respectability and gentility on middle-class women's employment has to be understood not only in its *own* analytical and theoretical context but against the background of the power of employers and of the labour market. It was not simply a question of persuading parliament of the justice of the cause; when it came to the question of employment, feminists had also to contend fully with the forces of a successful and expanding industrial capitalism which relied heavily on maintaining the separation of home and work for its successes. In such a context, their own modest successes are more convincing. They not only offered both encouragement and some job searching facilities through organizations and publications, but also sustained there some cogent critiques of male employment practices which, as in other areas, suggests a well-developed alternative feminist political philosophy. Moreover, the employment by the close of the century of well-known feminists in a number of new areas – government, medicine, and printing, for instance – was a concrete vindication of some forty years of tireless campaigning.

Notes and references

1 Women's Franchise League, *Report of Proceedings at the Inaugural Meeting*, London, 25 July 1889, p. 7. Speech of Chairman, Mrs Harriet McIlquham.

2 Patricia Branca, 'A New Perspective on Women's Work: A Comparative Typology', *Journal of Social History*, **9** (1975) pp. 129–53, (p. 147).

3 See Catherine Hall, 'The Early Formation of Victorian Domestic Ideology', in S. Burman (ed.), *Fit Work for Women* (London, 1979), pp. 15–31.

4 M.A., [Mabel Atkinson], *The Economic Foundations of the Women's Movement* (London, 1914), p. 11.

5 Mrs William [Maria] Grey, *Idols of Society; or Gentility and Femininity* (London, 1874), p. 11.

6 *Women and Work. A Weekly Industrial, Educational and Household Register for Women*, **47** (24 April 1875), p. 4.

7 Fawcett Library, London, Autograph Letter Collection, Letters of Lydia Becker, 23 March 1855.

8 *The Autobiography of Mary Smith, Schoolmistress and Nonconformist. A Fragment of Life* (London, 1892), p. 179.

9 *Life of Frances Power Cobbe by Herself*, 2 vols (London, 1894), II. 67.

10 Quoted in Margaret Todd, *The Life of Sophia Jex-Blake* (London, 1918), p. 69, 3 February 1859.

11 Anon., 'Benefit Societies for Women', *The Alexandra Magazine, and Englishwoman's Journal*, **1** (December 1864), pp. 47–54 (p. 48).

12 Grey, *Idols of Society*, p. 12.

13 Emily Faithfull, *On Some of the Drawbacks connected with the present Employment of Women* (2nd edition, London, 1862), p. 3.

14 Jessie Boucherett, 'The Employment of Women', *Nowadays* (1 July 1859), pp. 52–9 (p. 52).

15 'Association for Promoting the Employment of Women', *English Woman's Journal* (September 1860), p. 55.

16 Bye-Laws or Rules, Society for Promoting the Employment of Women.

17 F. K. Prochaska, *Women and Philanthropy in Nineteenth Century England* (Oxford, 1980), p. 31.

18 Boucherett, 'The Employment of Women', p. 53.

19 Jessie Boucherett, 'The Industrial Movement,' in Theodore Stanton (ed.), *The Woman Question in Europe* (London/New York, 1884), pp. 90–107 (p. 100).

20 Quoted in Anthea Callen, *Women in the Arts and Crafts Movement 1870–1914* (London, 1979), p. 189. William Lethaby to London County Council, n.d.

21 Quoted in Rosalie Silverstone, 'Office Work for Women: An Historical Review', *Business History*, **XVIII** (January 1976) I, pp. 98–110 (p. 101).

22 Hester Burton, *Barbara Bodichon* (London, 1949), p. 110.

23 Boucherett, 'The Employment of Women', p. 55.

24 Callen, *Women in the Arts and Crafts Movement*, p. 99.

25 Grey, *Idols of Society*, p. 15.

26 *Women Workers. The Official Report on the Conference held at Manchester, 1896, arranged by the National Union of Working Women.*

27 'Our Aim', *Women and Work. A Weekly Industrial, Educational and Household Register for Women*, **I** (6 June 1874), i, p. 4.

28 Margaret Bondfield, *A Life's Work* (London, 1949), p. 47.

29 Rose E. Squire, *Thirty Years in the Public Service. An Industrial Retrospect* (London, 1927), pp. 31–2.

30 Hilda Martindale, *From One Generation to Another. 1839–1944. A Book of Memoirs* (London, 1944), p. 73.

31 Helen Jones, *The First Women Factory Inspectors* (unpublished paper), p. 1. Anne Summers has pointed to a similar situation within nursing in her 'Pride and Prejudice: Ladies and Nurses in the Crimean War', *History Workshop Journal*, **16** (Autumn 1983), pp. 32–56.

32 Squire, *Thirty Years in the Public Service*, p. 39.

33 Jones, *The First Women Factory Inspectors*, p. 9.

33 Violet Markham, *May Tennant. A Portrait* (London, 1949), p. 21.

35 Jones, *The First Women Factory Inspectors*, p. 9.

36 A. Amy Bulley and Margaret Whitley, *Women's Work* (London, 1894), p. 23.

37 Bulley and Whitley, *Women's Work*, p. 23.

38 Elizabeth Garrett, *An Enquiry into the Character of the Contagious Diseases Acts of 1866–69* (London, 1870), p. 5.

39 Meredith Tax, *The Rising of the Women. Feminist Solidarity and Class Conflict, 1880–1917* (New York/London, 1980), p. 122.

40 Brian Harrison, 'Women's Health and the Women's Movement in Britain, 1840–1940', in Charles Webster (ed.), *Biology, Medicine and Society, 1840–1940* (Cambridge, 1981), pp. 15–71 (p. 45).

41 Grey, *Idols of Society*, p. 16.

42 The Liberal Education Act of 1870 introduced the principle of compulsory elementary schooling into Britain, thereby necessitating an increase in the numbers of teaching staff required. Between 1875 and 1914, the number of elementary school teachers rose from 23,656 to 165,901 (Lee Holcombe, *Victorian Ladies At Work. Middle Class Working Women in England and Wales 1850–1914* (Newton Abbot, 1973), p. 34).

43 Quoted in E. S. Riemer and J. C. Fout (eds), *European Women. A Documentary History. 1789–1945* (Brighton, 1983), p. 35; 'A Year's Experience in Women's Work', *English Woman's Journal* (October, 1861), pp. 112–17.

44 David Rubinstein, *Before the Suffragettes. Women's Emancipation in the 1890s* (Sussex, 1986), p. 80.

45 Bondfield, *A Life's Work*, p. 27.

46 Janet E. Courtney, *Recollected in Tranquillity* (London, 1926), p. 149.

47 Bulley and Whitley, *Women's Work*, p. 37.

Chronology

1841 Governesses' Benevolent Institution established.

1859 Society for Promoting the Employment of Women established.

1860 Nightingale Fund School of Nursing founded, St Thomas's Hospital, London.

1862 Female Middle Class Emigration Society established.
Female Medical Society (for midwives) established.

1864 *Alexandra Magazine* begins publication.

1865 Ladies' Medical College (for midwives) established.

1866 *Englishwoman's Review* begins publication.

1874 *Women and Work* begins publication.
Jane Nassau Senior appointed to workhouse inspectorate.

1875 Women clerks introduced, National Savings Bank.
Woman's Gazette begins publication.

1876 Women's clerical branch of Post Office introduced.

1880 *Work and Leisure* replaces *Woman's Gazette*.

1881   New Civil Service grade of woman clerk introduced.

1887   Royal British Nurses' Association founded.

1891   Women assistant commissioners appointed to Labour
       Commission.
       Women's Employment Defence League founded.

1893   First women factory inspectors appointed.

1899   Women Sanitary Officers' Association founded.

5 Trade, industry and organization: working-class women and work

The problems facing working-class women in industrial England were, in some ways, not as far removed from the needs of their middle-class sisters as we tend to imagine. At the level of financial need, their anxieties clearly overlapped and yet there were few concrete attempts at combination during this period. To all intents and purposes, the different classes in Victorian society occupied separate worlds and one of the major handicaps to really thorough feminist organization was recognized as having its roots in this division.

In the middle-class sector of campaigns around work, the stress was on the problems faced by the *single* woman with no other means of support. The growing demographic disparity between men and women was an issue of some concern in Victorian society; the 1851 census showed 1042 women for every 1000 men in the population and by 1901 a steady increase had led to 1068 women for every 1000 men.[1] The concerns within organizations dealing with working-class women took a different starting point. So many women in this broad economic bracket worked for wages, at least at some point in their lives, that issues such as working conditions and pay were more potent sources of need. In many ways, the issue of marital status remained important, though in a different context. Parliamentary and philanthropic commentators believed that women's waged work was leading to a crisis in the family by removing women from the domestic sphere ordained to them. The family – through this and other mechanisms such as the family wage – was thus a dominant consideration. And, in the case of widows, deserted wives and women whose husbands were unemployed, the consideration might be an urgent one if there were a family to feed, clothe and house. The intersection of class and gender was, as we noted in the previous chapter, even more acute in the working-class context where the question of respectability was likely to be a luxury that many women simply could not afford. Ellen Ross has commented on the preponderance of unskilled workers in London's adult male labour force in the 1890s, and the economic uncertainty that this spelt.[2]

The ideology of the separate spheres made little impact on working-class existence where economic necessity intervened, but it found an effective parallel in the sexual division of labour. The consistent and increasing relegation of women workers to poorly paid and low status jobs, both within the manual and the non-manual sectors of employment, effectively inhibited women's economic independence or prowess. The growing degree of state regulation of women's work further emphasized that the gender distinction was to remain an important feature of labour policies throughout this period.

In attempting to assess the numbers of working women at different times in the nineteenth century, we run up against a number of confusing problems. The change of work-base from the home to the workshop, factory or store as the site of production led to changing, though never fully clarified definitions of the meaning of words such as 'work', 'employment' and 'occupation'. In effect, 'work' became a shorthand for waged work, for gainful occupation, a prerogative, of course, of the public world. Clara Collet calculated that in 1901, 32 per cent of females in England and Wales over the age of 10 were occupied in areas other than home duties, and principally within some form of service industry (domestic service, retail trades, care of the sick, etc.), or in the textile industry.[3] Even at the time, the figures were challenged as inaccurate. 'It has been asserted that thousands of women who are in fact wage-earners did not so return themselves at the census, for different reasons; some because they did not consider it "genteel" thus to describe themselves.'[4]

Such speculations aside, the census designers were themselves unsure about just how to define economic activity. When the census of 1881 excluded unpaid household work as a category of gainful occupation, there was a dramatic drop in the female work rate figure from around 98 per cent (and almost the same as the work rate for men) to 42 per cent.[5] Unpaid household work – as distinct from waged domestic service, the largest employer of women in England – was largely the province of married women; a breakdown of the female labour force by marital status shows a high proportion of young single women and of widows in the public world of work and far smaller numbers of married women.

The peculiar anomaly of the woman-worker's career is that she starts at fourteen or fifteen in a world of profit-making and competitive industry, leaves it, and comes back to it again after the lapse of twenty-five years or so . . . while a man gives his best years to his industrial work, a woman gives precisely those years to other work, and therefore returns to industry under a considerable handicap.[6]

In reality, the married woman, seemingly occupied only in unpaid domestic labour within the private world of the conjugal home, frequently contributed to the family income through paid work which could be done in combination with her household labours, and which generally escaped the categories laid down in censuses. Many took in laundry or worked in the sweated trades where, as industrial out-workers, they could avoid problems such as the expense of child-minding. Throughout this period, countless women took in piecework to be done in their own home, work which could be picked up and put down according to the other demands on their time. Almost 71 per cent of the homeworkers in the London clothing trade in 1901 were women.[7] The low pay and the complete isolation which were the characteristics of this type of work rendered it virtually invisible, certainly within official statistical reckonings, but it none the less further blurs the definitional edges of terms such as 'work' and 'occupation'. As Patricia Branca has remarked, 'the history of formal employment must remain a minority theme in the social history of working-class women generally'.[8]

We cannot assume, however, that relinquishing formal paid employment upon marriage was always a matter of choice for women, notwithstanding the likelihood of a rapid pregnancy. Many occupations, though more particularly in what has come to be called the 'white-blouse' sector, imposed a marriage bar whereby automatic dismissal followed a woman's marriage. In effect, this gave employers constant access to younger and cheaper labour,[9] and at the same time upheld the dictates of separate sphere ideology whereby the paid labour of a married woman was equated with a husband's failure in fulfilling his role in the conjugal bargain.

'The measurement of a person's worth in terms of the money earned by the work performed' is, as Susan Kleinberg has stated, 'a fact of the modern industrial economy'.[10] It is also a succinct statement of separate sphere ideology which we can translate, at the economic level, into a distinction between exchange-value and use-value. Exchange-value is where labour is exchanged for wages and in its turn contributes to the making of profit; use-value is not exchangeable in this way and thus is not a *productive* capacity. While men produce, women reproduce:

here we have the root problem of the antagonism between use value and exchange value in its sharpest form. No one can deny that the service of the childbearing mother is that which is most indispensable to the continued existence of the nation and the State. But it is one which has no exchange value whatever.[11]

In effect, as we have seen, the distinction was not such a sharp one, as the consistency of female employment statistics illustrate. Working-class women worked in large numbers and often for a considerable proportion of their lives in both paid and unpaid positions, despite the howls of middle-class protest raised periodically in parliament and in the press against their involvement in the world of work.

For the most part, feminist activity in this area concentrated on the reality of the working woman's situation and on the necessity which brought it about, rather than on parading theoretical arguments in favour of or against women's work of this kind. It was for the most part a pragmatic and practical concern with the organization of benefit societies and unions, with working conditions and wages, with the evils and miseries of out-work which motivated organization within this stratum of society. Many of the organizations were run by interested middle-class women, though there is a significant working-class input as well. At one level, activists were, of course, feeding off other developments in the industrial sector which aided their work. Women's trade unions, for instance, tended to have their most marked successes in recruiting in periods when union activity in general was riding high. Thus, the Women's Protective and Provident League (WPPL) was established in 1874 at a time when men's unions were enjoying some success, both in membership terms and in establishing their legality. Similarly, it was in the brief period of 'new unionism' in the late 1880s and early 1890s when unskilled workers were being politicized for the first time that the Women's Industrial Council (WIC) and a score of women's unions were formed. Despite the indifference and even hostility of male unions, women were none the less able to ride the crest of their successes profitably.

The organization of women into trade unions was one of the two big issues which confronted feminists in this area in the second half of the nineteenth century. The other major question – and one which served to divide the feminist movement into at least two camps – was the issue of protective legislation, revived by government in the 1880s. Protective legislation hit at the heart of women's capacity to earn money and yet at the same time could offer significant improvements in conditions and hours of work. The dilemma for feminists was both a moral and a practical one, and dominated the agenda of most feminist-inspired organizations in this area in the later years of the century.

Organizationally, far more foundations were established by women in the working-class employment sphere than in the middle-class. The recognition was widespread that in working-class employments collective action such as that offered by unionization was more valuable than individual effort (as in campaigns within the male dominated professions). Combination and collectivity were the keynotes here, far more markedly than in, for instance, the Society for Promoting the Employment of Women (SPEW). Their form of organization and the preference they showed for such activity has certainly led modern historians to wonder whether in fact movements of working women in this period were indeed connected with feminist principles at all. Emma Paterson, founder of the WPPL, has been called 'more feminist than trade unionist' in a recent assessment of women's trades unionism, while the Fabian Mabel Atkinson found less 'sex-consciousness' among working women than middle-class women at the turn of the century.[12] The division between a feminist perspective and one which concerns itself with women's position and rights within the labour force seems an artificial one. The recognition, common to all these organizations, that women required separate bodies through which to conduct their campaigns, suggests they were fully conscious of the particular disabilities consequent upon their gender. None of the working-class women's organizations before the 1890s made female membership of male unions a plank of their policies; though they desired and won membership of the all-male Trades Union Congress (TUC), it was as representatives of women's groups that they did so. Moreover, the aim of organizing women from the working-classes was a directly political move, however 'moderate' the policies of particular organizations might be.

Sarah Boston is not wholly incorrect in her statement that much of the activity in this area was 'marked by a strange mixture of feminism, trade unionism and middle-class attitudes'.[13] She is, of course, noting not only the efforts of middle-class feminists on behalf of working women but also the philanthropic attitudes which sometimes carried over into such organizations. The prominence of active and socially assured feminists such as Lady Emilie Dilke, Clementina Black or Isabella Ford should not surprise us; nor should their backgrounds have prohibited them from the valuable work they did. Many of the activists, however, came from less elevated circles and many of them would have known the problems at first hand: Helen Blackburn was certainly not from a background of poverty or hardship but as the daughter of a civil engineer, she was unlikely to move in 'society' circles, although through her feminist connections she widened the net of her social opportunities, becoming a friend of both Lady Frances Balfour and the wealthy Jessie Boucherett; Amie Hicks, active in the East London Ropemakers Union, was the daughter of a Chartist; Emma Paterson worked as a bookbinder and married a cabinet-maker; all-round feminist Jeannette Wilkinson worked as an upholsteress from the age of 17. Their shared commitment was to give working women a voice in the public sphere, a voice which, despite their prominent role as labourers in that world, was denied them even more acutely than working men, and indeed all too often by those men.

For the most part, feminist activity was confined to umbrella organizations offering aid in establishing women's unions in specific trades. The WPPL saw this as its principal though not exclusive objective, and a trickle of other later organizations established during the rise of 'new unionism' had identical aspirations. Some were founded, in fact, by women critical of the League; the Women's Trade Union Association (WTUA) was begun in 1889 and its successor, the Women's Industrial Council (WIC) in 1894. There was also at least one society specifically organized around the controversial issue of protective legislation. The Women's Employment Defence League, headed by Boucherett, Blackburn and Ada Heather-Bigg, was founded in 1891 to fight any such legislative measures.

Before the foundation of the WPPL, no organization championing the cause of working women had existed. In the middle-class sphere, the problem was to find jobs for needy women and to render a new variety of occupations acceptable and accessible. Within the working classes, the problem was that of organization. A host of disincentives stood in the way of the successful unionization of women. Male unions at this stage were barely acceptable and themselves faced the problems of recruitment and of sustaining membership. The economic competition which women posed as a cheaper labour supply further determined the men not in unionizing women but in deterring their existence in the work-force. The 'family wage' was the most powerful mechanism whereby the combined force of male unionism and middle-class ideology 'colluded . . . to structure the working population along the lines of gender',[14] even where the woman worker had no male on whom she could rely economically. The whole thrust of the family wage was that male workers should earn sufficient themselves to provide for their family – wife and children – and thus remove the need for women to step outside the domestic world of home and family. It was a negotiating point which took no heed either of the notion of women's choice or of the countless women for whom an employed husband was one more myth alongside their own 'natural' role in the home – single women and widows, deserted wives and women whose husbands were invalids or out of work. In essence, the adoption of the family wage as a founding principle of wage bargaining was an act of hostility towards the working woman and hardly an encouragement to her unionization.

There were other factors too, besides the antagonism of male workers which limited the successes of female unions in this period. The sporadic tendency in women's work, interrupted by pregnancies and domestic duties, might, as we have already discussed, mean that in many cases work for women was simply a strategy for survival. Constant interruption added to poor pay and monotonous work would certainly not encourage women to invest energy in their identity as workers; their concentration in less skilled sectors of employment not only further discouraged any such identity but made them vulnerable too. Unskilled unions were late in taking off because such workers were, by virtue of their lack of skills, easily replaceable. Agitation could thus be easily nipped in the bud.

Women are inexperienced in combination and they entertain a lively and by no means groundless fear of the resentment of their employers . . . in many cases the attempt to form a combination among women meets with the open hostility of their employers. It is not uncommon for a woman who has undertaken the secretaryship of a union to be summarily dismissed.[15]

And their fears were rooted in grim reality. Giving evidence before the Royal Commission on Labour in the early 1890s, Clara James, an active London trade unionist, cited numerous instances of such intimidation. 'When the union was first started I was dismissed two days after I joined the union with two other girls.' James' evidence also spoke of employers who dismissed their employees even for attending union meetings.[16] Moreover, the high number of women whose source of income derived from occupations such as out-work or domestic service, where congregation with their peers was precluded, were without any means of organization. Many working women were isolated through their work and essentially untouchable in this organizational context.

Some more obvious and practical reasons prevented effective women's unions too. Where and when would they hold meetings? The traditional male meeting place of the pub made many women uneasy and women had no equivalent meeting place of their own, pushed back into family homes and excluded from public spaces as they were. Meetings could only be held out of working hours in this period, given the attitudes of employers to unions, but for many women, married and unmarried, those hours were taken up with domestic duties from which even involvement in paid work could not excuse them. It was against this background of improbable odds that the first really systematic steps to organize women as a separate entity within the work-force got under way, with the foundation of the WPPL in 1874.

The League's choice of name was a significant one, and its subsequent changes of name in 1889 and in 1891 were also important pointers to shifts in its policies. Both in its earliest days, and in its later phase, its principal function was to offer centralized assistance to working women in their own setting up of unions. It never was a trade union itself, nor claimed to be, but acted more as a mechanism for pooling funds, expertise and experience. It offered the sickness benefits with which both friendly societies and unions had long provided male workers, and a host of related activities. Reviewing the League's achievements in the previous decade, its house journal, the *Women's Union Journal*, noted, 'the library . . . Social Entertainments, a Co-operative Society, a Swimming Club, a Bank and a Loan Society, a Seaside Holiday House, the publication of this Journal'.[17] These were important provisions for they gave women access to activities and spaces from which they were often excluded; few banks, for example, would be willing to extend credit to a working woman, so the League was offering invaluable services and at the same time encouraging the autonomous development of a women's culture in this way. The accent placed on women's own achievements and impetus was an important one. Applauding the formation of the Rational Dress Society in 1881, the *Journal* noted, 'we rejoice to know [it] has at last been inaugurated, not by . . . any . . . male purveyor of fashions, but *by women*'.[18]

And yet its concentration on these areas of activity has been the centre of much criticism; the League has frequently been castigated for offering welfare instead of militancy.

It behoved the friends of the movement to walk guardedly, and to disarm suspicion until their cause had gained strength. The cumbrous title 'Women's Protective and Provident League' first adopted, directed attention accordingly to one side only of the work – that of insurance against sickness – while veiling its trade union aspect under the vague adjective 'protective'.[19]

The League was certainly not a militant organization in its early years, though it is difficult to see the basis on which it might have encouraged the militancy we associate with this form of political activity. The short lives of so many of the individual unions founded under its auspices were hardly encouraging in that respect. Male unions were still objects of suspicion in many quarters; the establishment of female unions which sanctioned not only a recognition of collective political ends for working people but also effectively the intrusion of women into the male world was a radical step in itself. As James Schmiechen has pointed out, the WPPL was far more of a propaganda and educational body 'wanting to acquaint working women with the principles and knowledge of unionism and to provide leadership in organizing unions'.[20] The League's tendency to cloak its activities in protestations of morality overlaid with philanthropy should not, however, obscure our understanding of its political significance.

There is frequent proof that men and women will starve to death upon honest labour (paid for, unfortunately, at dishonest prices) rather than apply for charitable or poor-law relief. The true way to help them seems to be induce them to help themselves; 'to make the weak strong to stand'.[21]

And yet, the mildness – even piety – of such a statement surely belies the reality of the active participation among women and the encouragement to autonomy which were the League's whole *raison d'être*.

Its gains were, as one might expect in such a climate, no more than modest. Its overall membership fluctuated wildly, though in 1884 there were less than a thousand women in its unions.[22] None the less in that time the League had succeeded, however temporarily, in organizing a number of London trades from boot and umbrella makers, tailoresses and laundresses to feather and flower workers and box makers. Nor were its activities confined wholly to London; various other industrial centres – Dewsbury and Leicester, for example – proved amenable if only in the short term.

The untimely death in 1886 of the diabetic Emma Paterson, who had founded the League, saw control pass into the hands of Lady Emilie Dilke. Dilke had taken a close interest in the WPPL's activities since she had first become a member in 1875 and she was a regular and generous contributor to its eternally ailing funds.[23] Under her leadership, and with two changes of nomenclature – from the Women's Trade Union and Provident League (1889) to the Women's Trade Union League (1891) – many of the former policies of the WPPL were abandoned and a more militant potential released. In what Gladys Boone has called the second phase of its history,[24] coinciding with the period of Dilke's leadership, the WTUL revamped its policies, abandoning its suspicion of both strike action and of protective legislation. At the same time, its stand as an all-women's organization was diluted primarily by the quest for more secure funding. Dilke introduced a scheme of affiliation applicable to unions with a female membership. In return for a fee of one halfpenny per female member per annum, affiliated unions could call on the WTUL for help in recruiting and organizing among women.

Attempts were also made to broaden the scope of the Union outside the metropolis, and at the time of its second and final change of name, the WTUL had seventeen London unions and six provincial affiliates. Its journal too underwent some transformation. It became the *Women's Trade Union Review*, quarterly rather than weekly. Despite the more hard-hitting approach which Dilke introduced, the old spirit of philanthropic cheer was not entirely quenched:

At the gathering of February 16th, Miss Routledge gave a short address on the benefit side of Trades Unionism, pointing out the good effects of Trade Societies in encouraging thrift. . . . Two ladies gave charming recitations, and several sang.[25]

The 1890s saw both a growth in women's trade union membership and the establishment of several new women's organizations similar to the union, though it remained the most prominent and the largest. The WTUA of 1889 was founded by women who had grown dissatisfied with the stance of the WTUL, amongst them Clementina Black, Amie Hicks, Clara James (the new organization's secretary) and Florence Balgarnie. The aims of the new association differed little from its more established parent and though it enjoyed some success in organizing unions, it was to be a short-lived venture. It merged in 1897 with the Women's Industrial Council, then three years old and already employing to the full the capacities of the most prominent members of the WTUA. The WIC had established itself from the outset as a watchdog body principally interested in research and educational activities. It made no attempts to build women's unions but defined its aim as 'to watch over women engaged in trades, and all industrial matters which concern women'.[25] It carefully distinguished trades from professions and distanced itself from any official interest in the latter. It placed considerable emphasis too on the recreational facilities it aimed to provide alongside its more academic function.

The Women's Industrial Council was established by a little group of people, who after several years' endeavour to organize working women had become convinced, 1st: that there was great need for the careful and systematic collection and publication of facts about the condition of women's work, and 2nd: that the position of working women might be ameliorated in various ways by the organizing of recreative clubs, by the training and development of greater skills in certain occupations, and in some instances by alterations of the law.[27]

The Council thus combined the non-union activities of the early WPPL with many of the roles of the middle-class Society for Promoting the Employment of Women. Ellen Mappen has dubbed the WIC a product of what she calls 'social feminism', a movement in which women's economic and social position were given as much attention and credence as the campaign for the parliamentary vote.[28] Many of the WIC's members were women whose political involvements spanned both party politics *and* feminist lobbies, though the council itself, in keeping with many feminist pressure groups of the period, boasted 'no restrictions of creed or political party'.[29] Its active membership in these early years comprised those women who had found even the restyled WTUL too flaccid in its policies.

The formation of the various organizations was helped, of course, by shifts in the political and economic climate which made the concerns and efforts of workers' organizations both more prominent and more acceptable. All these bodies grew up not just in the wake of the 'new unionism' prompted by the famous London Dock Strike of 1889 but by the successful action some months earlier of the women at London's Bryant and May match factory. The success of what is known – belittlingly – as the Match Girls' Strike had, not surprisingly, produced a spate of union activity elsewhere: the organized women's union movement in Liverpool was greatly boosted by the success of the strike, and in 1890 a women Coat Makers Union successfully struck for reduced hours.[30] Lady Dilke had estimated that in 1870 around 57,800 women were members of trade unions; by 1896 that figure had risen to 117,888.[31] The figure represents some 7.8 per cent of all union members.[32] The larger proportion of unionized women were within the textile industry, and more particularly in the cotton trade. Textiles were one of the chief employers of female labour, women often outnumbering the male operatives. 'About four times as many women are employed in textiles alone as in teaching.'[33] This was an area, too, in which women had for many years been incorporated in mixed unions. It was, moreover, far more common for married women to retain full-time paid employment in these areas of work than in any other.

It was in the north-west of England, where the preponderance of textiles was so obvious, that another influential educational and campaigning women's organization found a large body of its support. Inaugurated in 1883, the Women's Co-operative Guild (WCG), an off-shoot of the larger co-operative movement, made the improvement of the condition of women one of its stated aims. Numerically it enjoyed a rapid success; by 1893 almost 6500 women had joined it and branches existed all over the country. In common with the other organizations, the Guild combined the practical politics of co-operation – coal and clothing clubs, maternity bags – with longer term campaigning for women's suffrage and enquiries into working women's conditions: as Jean Gaffin has put it, the WCG's concerns ranged 'from loyalty to the local store to the white slave traffic'.[34]

In common with most of the organizations dealing with the problems and needs of working-class women, the leadership of the WCG was a mixed bag of both interested middle-class and working-class women. The Guild had been started by Alice Sophia Acland, the comfortably off wife of an Oxford academic. Margaret Llewellyn Davies, niece of educationalist Emily Davies, was another middle-class activist. Her family's involvement in Christian Socialism had led her into the Guild in its earliest days and by the end of the 1880s she had become its general secretary. The Guild's historian, on the other hand, was the daughter of an artisan. Catherine Webb had been brought up in a Co-operative family and retained strong connections with the movement throughout her life. And in Bolton, it was textile worker Sarah Reddish who moved from presidency of her local WCG branch to the central committee and a full-time organizing post with the Guild. The WCG had connections, too, with other women's organizations and individuals, especially the WTUA. Clementina Black was a strong supporter, as was Clara Collet from the Board of Trade. The WCG collaborated with Collet in investigating the statistics of women's work.[35]

The common characteristic of all these organizations is their concern with the singularity of women's position and women's requirements in the worlds of work and leisure, and even within the working-class home. These spheres could not be divorced given the disrupted employment patterns caused by, for instance, child-rearing, which governed the lives of so many women. Although their principal concerns remained, for the most part, the organization of women either within an industrial or at least a public context, the wider feminist implications of that activity and of its inevitable connection with feminist lobbying in other areas of concern never escaped their attention. Even when the WTUL opted for a policy of encouraging women into unions of mixed rather than single-sex membership in the 1890s, other specifically female issues remained central planks of their overall philosophy. Given the extensive nature of women's oppression, feminist activity was necessarily split into a series of autonomous but linked campaigns.

One area in which many feminists involved largely in other areas of protest *did* become enmeshed in working-class issues was over the thorny question of the rights and wrongs of protective legislation. Legislative measures which restricted or prohibited women's work in certain fields or limited their duties or hours of labour had featured prominently in the social reforms of the 1830s and 1840s in particular. Angela John has suggested that interest in this early phase of protective legislation in women's labour grew largely out of an initial preoccupation with the effects of work on children.[36] When the issue was revived in the mid 1880s with women's employment as its primary target the political scene was of a very different complexion. Most importantly for our interests here, the strength and articulacy of organizations representing various factions of women's interests became involved in debating the ethics of this issue and, indeed, in lobbying parliament. In the event, the country's legislators paid little attention to such lobbying, feminist or otherwise; state intervention in areas of social and economic concern was a growing reality despite the voices raised in protest by the proponents of individualism. The extension of the factory inspectorate to a workable level and its final embracing of women inspectors signalled a more serious intention of enforcement on the part of government than had the early permissive acts.

The issue was a sensitive and explosive one for feminists, dividing them – surprisingly – less along class lines than along lines of political belief. There was no simple division, as some commentators have suggested, between middle-class opponents of the legislation and working-class supporters, nor between the middle-class women as voicing a 'bourgeois' politics and working-class women a 'socialist' preference.[37] Three positions emerged in the debate: the outright laissez-faire opposition to any proposals

as a restriction on women's freedom; those supporters who saw
restriction as a progressive and humane response of the state; and
those – more numerous than the unqualified supporters – who
applauded the principle of protective legislation but only where
its application was not on the basis of gender. The critics, without
exception, also pointed to the corollary of political with economic
powerlessness which they felt such legislation spelt out. Much of
the debate, of course, was conducted by women for whom any
acts would be no more than a theoretical erosion of liberty or
extension of humanitarianism; inevitably we have far less access
to the attitudes of women workers themselves, though groups
such as the women surface workers at the coal mines did organize
their opposition, supported by the anti-legislation feminists
grouped around the *Englishwomen's Review*.[38]

For working women in targeted industries, such legislation
could, of course, mean the difference between wages, however
arduously or unpleasantly earned, and unemployment; for the
defiant 'pit-brow lasses' it was a second round in the struggle.
Forced out of underground mine work by an earlier chapter of
legislation, they were now confined to poorer paid surface work.
David Rubinstein has suggested that the attitudes of working-class
women to state regulation was mixed but 'that there is little doubt
that the impact of government reform was an unwelcome reality
for many late Victorian and Edwardian working people'.[39] Barrett
and McIntosh have pointed out, however, that while for some
women regulation of hours or exclusion from specific trades might
threaten their livelihood, others perhaps welcomed the shorter
working day or the release from the double burden of industrial
and domestic duties.[40] Speculations aside, the silence of women
workers reflects both the weakness of their unions in campaigning
on this issue, for or against, and their total neglect by the
legislators.

A Departmental Committee is appointed to consider whether a certain
trade is dangerous. There is no rule requiring that the women in the
trade should be represented in the Committee, and it is a fact that they
are not represented.[41]

The significant point is that women were legislated *for*, without
consultation; feminists of all opinions were quick to pick up on
the wider implications of this total neglect of their views.

The highest welfare of the race can only be attained when women share fully the privileges and responsibilities of men. Equality under factory legislation is one step towards the ideal. It does not seem probable that it can be attained so long as women remain voteless, so long as women are political non-entities, counting for nothing in the eyes of the legislators, or at least only considered when the claims of men with votes have been satisfied.[42]

This feminist perspective was entirely correct in its assessment; it not only hinted at the conjunction of existing political and potential economic disfranchisement, but also at the need to examine the motives for protective legislation separately from its effects. Regulatory labour legislation of this sort could, of course, be conceived in at least two different ways. Was its intention to protect the health and safety of women workers? Or was it intended to prevent them from competing for jobs with men who, after all, were now largely enfranchised? Is it even possible to tease out the conflicting strands of humanitarianism and economic manipulation which such opposing motives suggest? Parliament was doubtless as divided as the feminist movement on this.

Some women saw such legislation as the 'ratification by the State of the will of the people'[43] while others concentrated on its effects in 'diminishing the self-dependence of the worker'.[44] There was clearly a need in nineteenth-century England to curb the worst excesses of employers whose interpretation of the free market economy was detrimental to the health and safety of their workers. Women from markedly different political camps found agreement on this principle. Writing to the Liberal – indeed by this time Liberal-Unionist – Millicent Fawcett, Edith Pechey Phipson asserted that, 'These regulations are a good example of the way in which men legislate for women. Of course if the government chooses to restrict the hours of working for the whole mill that is a different matter.'[45] Her view coincided with that of socialist feminist Enid Stacy. 'A very great injustice . . . will be done women if State interference deals with them intimately and leaves men pretty much alone. Socialists urge that the State has power to regulate individuals *qua* individuals, but not *qua* women.'[46]

Women's trade unions had little industrial muscle with which to challenge working hours and the like, and it was into this gap that the state stepped. The philanthropic and ideological motives which had fuelled the earliest attempts at protective legislation remained apparent, but the corresponding increase in the voice of the male labour force may well have added a further dimension to government motives. After all, the new Factory Acts applied only in areas of mixed employment. The act of 1878 specifically exempted workplaces exclusively employing women. The sweated trades so heavily worked by women were also untouched.

There was not much to choose, for example – if our criteria is [sic] risk to life or health – between work in the mines, and work in the London dressmaking trades. But no one suggested that sweated needlework should be prohibited to women.[47]

And it was upon this unevenness that even the feminist proponents of legislation commented. Just as they had noted the curious logic of deeming nursing a feminine occupation but that of the doctor unsuitable (see Chapter 4), almost identical inconsistencies in this area were emphasized.

It is noticeable that legislative restrictions on women's work are purely class legislation. No legislator has yet attempted to make laws which shall prevent women from taking night work when nursing, or acting, or dancing. No one has yet proposed to restrict the number of hours given to her work overtime by the female teacher in an elementary or secondary school.[48]

The occupations which Brownlow chooses to cite here are, of course, all overwhelmingly female in composition. Her silent point is, again, that the acts provided for the restriction of women's labour only in areas worked also by men.

There are, according to the Census, 185,246 women employed in the 'washing and bathing service,' and only 6,912 men; but those few men have far more political power than the nearly 200,000 women, who have absolutely none, and the same may be said of every trade in which men and women engage. The political power is always with the men, so that it is most difficult for members of the House of Commons to withstand the demands made by the men of any trade for Acts of Parliament to restrict or prohibit the employment of women in that trade.[49]

And the Central Committee of the National Society for Women's Suffrage sent a memorial to the Home Secretary in 1887 to the effect that it was 'unjust for a Parliament, in the election of which women have no votes to interfere with the right of women to work'.[50]

Many of the most staunch opponents of the acts were to be found among that group of older feminists most closely associated with the cause of suffrage – Jessie Boucherett, Lydia Becker, Millicent Garrett Fawcett – rather than among the new generation of women active specifically in employment, such as Gertrude Tuckwell or Clementina Black. David Rubinstein has even suggested that the pro-legislation women sought to distance themselves from the feminist movement. He cites Beatrice Webb as well as Black and Tuckwell as examples, and though Webb certainly voiced a hostility to feminism (which she regretted in later life) it is hard to see that tendency in either Black or Tuckwell, both far more centrally concerned with *women* than was Webb.[51] Despite the cogency of their argument in the specifically political context, opponents of regulation found themselves in something of an impasse thanks to their adherence to theories of liberal individualism. In championing women's rights to all available employment, they came close to sanctioning work which clearly endangered health and safety. The white lead trade, with its high mortality rate, was one which had haunted the Victorian conscience for many years. And yet Jessie Boucherett and her colleagues, who through the SPEW were fighting these sorts of conditions, saw it as the preferable option for many women.

We were told that in Newcastle this plan of forbidding women's work in lead factories would mean loss of employment for eight hundred women, and there was nothing to take its place. No alternative but the work-house – or worse.[52]

At no stage, then, was there clear agreement within the movement as to the ethics of such legislation. Where there *was* a coming together of opinions it was on the subordination and powerlessness which was emphasized by the legislation. 'Women, already handicapped by social prejudice and lack of training, are further hindered by unequal legislation.'[53]

Working-class women were at the bottom of the economic pile, forced *into* distasteful jobs by economic necessity and forced *out* of them by the ethics and desires of another class and another gender. And if there is less apparent political activity arising from these women and more on their behalf from their middle-class sisters, we should not be too surprised.

The huge gap between the experiences and lives of people in the different classes of Victorian society meant that the efforts of interested middle-class feminists would not always reflect or coincide with the needs and desires of working-class women, though there can be no doubt that such shrewd investigators as Clara Collet or Helen Blackburn, as well as the new women factory inspectors, were well acquainted with working conditions at the very least. These organizations reflect rather the opinions and judgements of women utterly inexperienced in these matters, however sympathetic they might have been. In consequence, we see no campaigns around the appalling conditions of much domestic service, which employed so large a proportion of the female labour force throughout the century. Nor is there much interest shown in women's agricultural labour despite government investigations in this area in the 1840s. Feminism in this period was a wholly urban movement, clustered for the most part around the larger towns where industrial conditions were easily observable.

The interest shown by so many better-off women in tackling the problems of industrial conditions and practices rather than the home lives of working women, and their choice of organizations supporting autonomous development rather than the host of phil-anthropic societies offering practical succour tinged with moralism, is significant. We cannot write off middle-class feminists in this area as philanthropists *manqué* nor set up an inevitable tension between feminism and trade unionism. As Sheila Rowbotham has said, 'Class tensions are certainly present when working-class women combine with middle-class ones. But there is no universal historical law which decrees that the interests of the working-class women will always be subordinated.'[54] There were instances in which feminist organizations voiced directly the stated needs of working-class women. The lobbying which preceded the appointment of female factory inspectors is one such example; both working-class women through the TUC and labour organizations and bodies such as the WPPL and WTUA campaigned around this issue, as did middle-class societies such as the SPEW. There were few other ways in which concerned middle-class women could understand the problems which divided them from their working-class sisters without falling into the trap of philanthropy. Despite the mistakes, the failures, the occasional lapses into a Sunday-school ambience, feminist organizations in this central area of working-class women's work represent a serious attempt at broadening the notion of sisterhood beyond – or perhaps in spite of – the parameters of class.

Notes and references

1 B. R. Mitchell and Phyllis Deane, *Abstract of British Historical Statistics* (Cambridge, 1962), p. 6.

2 Ellen Ross, ' "Fierce Questions and Taunts": Married Life in Working-Class London, 1870–1914'. *Feminist Studies*, **8** (1982) 3, pp. 575–602 (p. 576).

3 Clara Collet, *Women in Industry* (London, n.d.), p. 4.

4 B. L. Hutchins, *Statistics of Women's Life and Employment* (privately printed, 1909), p. 11.

5 Catherine Hakim, 'Census Reports As Documentary Evidence: The Census Commentaries 1801–1951,' in *Sociological Review*, **28** (August 1980), 3, pp. 551–80 (p. 560); see, too, Eric Richards, 'Women in the British Economy since about 1700: An Interpretation,' *History*, **lix** (1974), pp. 337–57.

6 B. L. Hutchins, *Statistics of Women's Life*, p. 15.

7 James A. Schmiechen, *Sweated Industries and Sweated Labour. The London Clothing Trades 1860–1914* (London, 1984), p. 71.

8 Patricia Branca, 'A New Perspective on Women's Work: A Comparative Typology,' *Journal of Social History*, **9** (1975), pp. 129–53 (p. 147).

9 Jane Lewis, *Women in England 1870–1950: Sexual Divisions and Social Change* (Sussex/Bloomington, Indiana, 1984), pp. 173; 186.

10 Susan J. Kleinberg, 'The Systematic Study of Urban Women', in Milton Cantor and Bruce Laurie (eds), *Class, Sex and the Woman Worker* (London/Westport, Connecticut, 1977), pp. 20–42 (p. 23).

11 B. L. Hutchins, *Conflicting Ideals: Two Sides of the Woman's Question* (London, 1913), p. 11.

12 Dame Anne Godwin, 'Early Years in the Trade Unions', in Lucy Middleton (ed.), *Women in the Labour Movement. The British Experience* (London, 1977), pp. 94–112 (p. 95); M.A., [Mabel Atkinson], *The Economic Foundations of the Women's Movement* (London, 1914), p. 15.

13 Sarah Boston, *Women Workers and the Trade Union Movement* (London, 1980), p. 31.

14 Michèle Barrett and Mary McIntosh, 'The "family wage" ', in E.

Whitelegg *et al.* (eds), *The Changing Experience of Women* (Oxford, 1982), pp. 71–87 (p. 74).

15 A. Amy Bulley and Margaret Whitley, *Women's Work* (London, 1894), p. 83.

16 Parliamentary Papers, House of Commons, 1892, XXXV, Royal Commission on Labour, p. 342.

17 *Women's Union Journal*, **132** (January 1887), XII.

18 *Women's Union Journal*, **73** (February 1882), VII, p. 9.

19 Bulley and Whitley, *Women's Work*, p. 70.

20 Schmiechen, *Sweated Industries*, pp. 84–5.

21 *Women's Union Journal*, **72** (January, 1882) VII, p. 3.

22 Teresa Olcott, 'Dead Centre: The Women's Trade Union Movement in London, 1874–1914', *London Journal*, **2** (1976) 1, pp. 33–50 (p. 40).

23 Norbert C. Soldon, *Women in British Trade Unions 1874–1976*, (Dublin, 1978), p. 27.

24 Gladys Boone, *The Women's Trade Union Leagues in Great Britain and the United States of America* (New York, 1942), p. 26.

25 *Women's Trade Union Review* n.d. [April 1891] 1, p. 75.

26 Women's Industrial Council pamphlet, n.d.

27 *The Women's Industrial News* (October 1895). Specimen number.

28 Ellen Mappen, *Helping Women at Work. The Women's Industrial Council 1889–1914* (London, 1985), pp. 11–12.

29 *The Women's Industrial News* (October 1895).

30 Soldon, *Women in British Trade Unions*, pp. 30–1.

31 Soldon, *Women in British Trade Unions*, pp. 28; 46.

32 David Rubinstein, *Before the Suffragettes. Women's Emancipation in the 1890s* (Sussex, 1986), pp. 124–5.

33 B. L. Hutchins, *Statistics of Women's Life and Employment*, p. 26.

34 Jean Gaffin, 'Women and Co-operation', in Lucy Middleton, *Women in the Labour Movement*, pp. 113–42 (p. 137).

35 Catherine Webb, *The Woman with the Basket. The History of the Women's Co-operative Guild 1883–1927* (Manchester, 1927), p. 108.

36 Angela John, *By the Sweat of their Brow. Women Workers at Victorian Coal Mines* (2nd edition, London, 1984), p. 148.

37 Hal Draper and Anne G. Lipow, 'Marxist Women versus Bourgeois Feminism', *Socialist Register*, **13** (1976), pp. 178–226.

38 Angela John, *By the Sweat of their Brow*, p. 148.

39 Rubinstein, *Before the Suffragettes*, pp. 148; 139.

40 Barrett and McIntosh, in Whitelegg (ed.), *The Changing Experience of Women*, pp. 75–6.

41 Jessie Boucherett, Helen Blackburn and some others, *The*

Condition of Working Women and the Factory Acts (London, 1896), p. 23.

42   Jane M. E. Brownlow, *Women and Factory Legislation* (London, 1896), p. 7.

43   Bulley and Whitley, *Women's Work*, p. 168.

44   Boucherett, Blackburn, *et al.*, *The Condition of Working Women*, p. 76.

45   Fawcett Library, London, Autograph Letter Collection: Women's Movement 1888–96. Edith Pechey Phipson to Millicent Garrett Fawcett, 6 December 1891.

46   Enid Stacy, 'A Century of Women's Rights', in Edward Carpenter (ed.), *Forecasts of the Coming Century by a decade of Writers* (Manchester, 1897), pp. 86–101 (p. 98).

47   Sally Alexander, 'Women's Work in Nineteenth-Century London; A Study of the Years 1820–50', in Juliet Mitchell and Ann Oakley (eds), *The Rights and Wrongs of Women* (Harmondsworth, 1976), pp. 59–111 (p. 63).

48   Brownlow, *Women and Factory Legislation*, p. 4.

49   Boucherett, Blackburn, *et al.*, *The Condition of Working Women*, pp. 21–2.

50   Quoted in Angela John, *By the Sweat of their Brow*, p. 148.

51   Rubinstein, *Before the Suffragettes*, p. 111.

52   Boucherett, Blackburn, *et al.*, *The Condition of Working Women*, p. 80.

53   Brownlow, *Women and Factory Legislation*, p. 6.

54   Sheila Rowbotham, Introduction to *The Daughters of Karl Marx. Family Correspondence 1866–98* (London, 1982), pp. xvii–xl, (p. xxxvi).

Chronology

1857–8   Select Committee on employment of women and children in bleaching and dyeing trades.

1867   Workshop Act.

1868   Report of Royal Commission on Employment of Children, Young Persons and Women in Agriculture.

1869   Bleaching and Dyeing Act.

1874   Women's Protective and Provident League founded.
National Union of Women Workers founded.
Union of Women in Bookbinding founded.

1875   Union of Women Upholsteresses founded.
Union of Women Shirt and Collar Makers founded.

1876 First accredited women delegates attend Trades Union Congress: Emma Paterson and Edith Simcox.
Women's Union Journal (WPPL organ) begins publication.
Women's Printing Society founded.
Report of Royal Commission on Factories and Workshops.

1877 Tailoresses' Union founded.
East London Tailoresses' Union founded.

1878 Women's Halfpenny Bank instituted.
Women's Union Swimming Club established.
Factory and Workshop Act.

1881 Working Women's Benefit Society founded in Oxford.

1882 London Women's Trades Council established.
Municipal Workwomen's Society founded.
Report to House of Commons on White Lead Works.

1883 Factory and Workshop Act.
Women's Co-operative Guild founded.

1888 Bryant and May women workers' strike (match girls' strike).

1889 WPPL becomes Women's Trade Union and Provident League.
Women's Trade Union Association founded.

1891 WTUPL becomes Women's Trade Union League; *Women's Union Journal* becomes *Women's Trade Union Review*.
Factory and Workshop Act.

1894 Labour Commission report on women's employment.
Report on Condition of Labour in Lead Industries.
Women's Industrial Council founded.

1895 Factory and Workshop Act.

1898 *Women's Industrial News* (WIC organ) begins publication.

1899 Seats for Female Shop Assistants Act.

6   Marriage and morality

Both feminist campaigners and the ideologues of Victorian respectability placed much emphasis on the value and importance of rigorous and well-defined moral standards as a means of ordering society. The popular and widespread assumption that this moral code spelt a reluctance to articulate ideas about sexuality and a retreat into prudish euphemism or silence is correct in only one respect; the increasing tendency to equate moral values pre-eminently with codes of sexual behaviour. The elision of sexuality and morality in this period is important in hinting at the central areas of fear and concern within Victorian society; interest in matters sexual was not so much repressed as subjected to attempts at manipulation and control. Alongside the extension in discussions of sexuality, often refracted through anxieties over, for instance, the sexual statistics of birth and marriage, or in a concern over workplace morality, we can trace an increasing profile of intervention on the part of the state.

Early Victorian governments had expressed horror over reports of the moral degradation consequent upon women's work in mixed environments. Royal Commissions and other investigative bodies were initiated, though the tentative nature of the ensuing legislation meant scant implementation of their recommendations. By the later years of the nineteenth century, however, the state felt confident to intervene in more 'private' areas of morality, legislating on the sexual preferences of individuals and on marital relations. Marriage and divorce, venereal disease, prostitution, male homosexuality, contraception and incest all became areas of judicial attention in the later nineteenth century.

The state's role in legislating within the 'private' sphere poses interesting questions regarding its part in maintaining or creating sexual inequalities. The point was not lost on contemporary feminists who were tireless in voicing the opinion that a male parliament would inevitably articulate the needs and desires of men in every sphere. The legal process was clearly a powerful mechanism whereby men and women could be written into their separate spheres. The values of respectability, of social and sexual purity which were deemed the 'natural' preferences of women, were upheld stringently in legislation affecting the areas of personal and indeed of public morality.[1]

Victorian perceptions of sexuality – the subject of a vast literature ranging from medical textbooks and religious tracts to the successful industry of pornography – were built around a fundamental belief in sexual difference. Women and men were categorized by their biology and that biology was seen as central in determining their social roles. Many modern writers have pointed to the collusion of the medical profession, acting as 'social engineers',[2] in determining a relationship between biology and sexual and social behaviour. Where women in earlier times had been widely regarded as the lustful sex whose tempting, seducing sexuality represented man's downfall from the biblical tale of Eve on, the keynote of nineteenth-century English attitudes is the passivity and reluctant sexuality of women, or at least of respectable women. We are concerned here, of course, not so much with the reality of women's and men's lives as with the ideology which pervaded their relations with one another.

Separate sphere ideology, with its division of public and private, had its sexual connotations and ramifications. Its association with religious values and with women's moral guardianship polarized perceptions of a female sexuality awakened principally by the procreative urge and a male sexuality, active, dominant and powerful. And it is this question of power, of course, which is, as so many theorists have shown, the central point. Nineteenth-century feminists drew parallels between men's political and sexual power; there was every likelihood that the woman who became involved in campaigns around suffrage or work or education would be at the very least sympathetic to the ideas propounded by feminists concerned primarily with this sphere of the moral. The inextricable links between them were pointed out time and time again: biological characteristics came to determine a division of labour by gender and a separate curriculum for the education of boys and girls. Medical men intoned the dangers to a woman's productive capacities produced by higher education.

Martha Vicinus has noted that 'our social and psychological structuring of sex is congruent with and influenced by the rise of industrial capitalism'.[3] The timing of this new approach to female sexuality corresponds largely to the period in which fundamental economic changes were also occurring. The separation of home and workplace, which was the gradual requirement of an increasingly factory-based technological economy, was the physical expression of the separate spheres. Women were, at least in theory, confined within the domestic space mapped out by the parental or marital home. In moral terms, the public world of work was dirty, brutal and often immoral (hence concerns over female participation) while the home, the domain of the woman, signified peace and purity. The sexual articulation of that polarity had an irresistible logic: man's sexuality was active, often violent and certainly dominant, a mirror of his public involvements, while that of woman was circumscribed by the demands of purity. Her distaste for public activity was matched by an antipathy for active sexual relations. At the same time, that ordering proved invaluable as a means of justifying women's exclusion from the workforce (which in reality meant low pay in monotonous casual jobs) and of providing a means of divorcing production as the definitive male and reproduction as the definitive female capacity.

This constant and potent overlap between moral economy and political economy made the area of morality a crucial site for feminist attack. Their intrusion into public spheres – employment, political recognition, government – had been shocking enough in itself. This sphere, which involved their transgressing the private and bringing it into a public arena, was in itself a radical statement. The unimpeachable personal respectability of many of the most vocal campaigners – Josephine Butler, Millicent Fawcett, Frances Power Cobbe – lent their campaigns a strength which often bewildered their opponents. Theirs was a radicalism intensified not only by their public pronouncements on private issues and as women but by the stability of their own personal reputations.

Feminist campaigning in this arena centred on inequalities and problems relating to the institution of marriage and on efforts to wipe out a double standard of morality based on gender, which licensed male freedom and female suppression. The two areas were, of course, linked by the legitimation of the double standard enshrined in matrimonial legislation. The high incidence of marriage and its centrality in women's lives, determining their status whether they married or not, made it an obvious and important feminist concern. Campaigners embraced the property of married women, their access to divorce, custody of children, violence within marriage and the curious controversy over marriage to a deceased wife's sister.

All these issues, along with that of prostitution, were areas of parliamentary attention throughout this period. Growth in population and in corresponding preference for urban living had mobilized the increasing degree of state intervention into the private lives of its citizens. Sanitation and housing, water supplies and the control of disease, all became subject to government directive in some way during the nineteenth century, alongside the crossover from the definably public to the obviously private. Government's role became an increasingly prescriptive one in this context, laying down acceptable sexual behaviour and policing sexual relations through laws governing such areas as prostitution, homosexuality or contraception. In many respects, the state assumed the role played in earlier periods by the church; in its sanctioning of marriage and its pronouncements as to the grounds on which divorce was valid, in its defining the forms of licit and illicit sexual behaviour, in its treatment of prostitution, it was as much a moral governing body as religions had been in other ages or as they were in other cultures.

The high profile involvement of feminists in all areas of moral injustice dated from the earliest years of organization; in the 1850s Barbara Leigh Smith had published a tract on women's legal disabilities and was one of those active in an early committee for changing the law on married women's property. As the movement grew in numbers and in confidence, and as its analysis of the position of women grew more sophisticated, so it widened its net. The property of married women was quite obviously an important issue, but critics have often wrongly dismissed the campaign as beneficial merely to small numbers of wealthy women. Within a decade, however, that campaigning platform was only one of several and by the 1880s, women were openly and publicly debating the sexual *mores* of their society. In part, their growing analytical rigour fuelled not just their sharp sense of injustice but often that of fear too.

Much of the moral stance which late Victorian feminists assumed stemmed from fear. Linda Gordon and Ellen DuBois have noted that feminist attitudes to sexuality revolve largely around the *dangers* it implied, and in her study of the Ripper murders of autumn 1888, Judith Walkowitz has argued that the sensationalist reporting which accompanied the five murders and the ensuing fruitless enquiry 'established a common vocabulary and iconography of male violence'.[4] Feminists at the time pointed out that these 'womenkillings', however horrific, were structured into the accepted relations between men and women.[5] And the sexual nature of these crimes seemed obvious to them; the victims were poor women and women known to have had recourse to prostitution.

Campaigns around marital violence pre-dated the murders by a full decade and one of the most powerful arguments that campaigners against 'wife-torture' had in their armoury was the inadequacy of the law in protecting women from reprisal. Frances Power Cobbe maintained that fear of brutal retaliation inhibited women from taking their grievances to the police or from sustaining complaints. In her influential article on marital assault in the *Contemporary Review* of 1878, Cobbe recounted the grisly tale of 'a woman who appeared without a nose, and told the magistrate she had *bitten it off herself!*'[6]

Cobbe and many others were convinced that levels of male violence were vastly exacerbated by the consumption of alcohol; it was not an analysis exclusive to feminists, as long-standing mixed temperance societies show. Women were, however, as Ethel Snowden pointed out, 'the greatest sufferers from the drink habit'[7] – hence the high incidence of temperance activity among feminists. The crimes and fears induced by drunkenness were not limited, however, to physical assault. For many women, economic hardship constituted a frequent nagging fear; the economic dependency defined as the normal marital state made it difficult for women to leave violent husbands.

The moral stance which characterized the feminist position should be understood against a background tinged with both economic and physical threats as well as with theoretical objections to legislative or even cultural injustices. Their criticisms and their solutions encompassed a broad understanding of the moral world; sexual inequality was simply one expression among many of the repression they suffered.

They saw themselves as victims of a male ideology, as victims of a lust denied to them, of a right to speak denied to them, of a society shaped by male requirements. The very notion of justice, they felt, had been perverted; a recourse to moral superiority was an obvious and logical position, more especially given the role ordained them by that ideology. Feminists took hold of the position to which they were limited by Victorian ideology and inverted its precepts, turning the duties of moral guardianship into a crusade which castigated the laxity and degradation of precisely those who ascribed to them that role. Where involvement in feminist politics might lead to some loss of caste, the retention and proclamation of the qualities of moral virtue as the founding principles of that feminism confounded the image; the religiosity which many of these women maintained, their adherence to temperance and to many of the other mainstream values espoused by the ideology which confined them became a distinctive source of power. Alex Tyrrell has shown that early women temperance activists in the 1830s had advised female supporters to reject marriage proposals from men who were not teetotal, a practice which hit at the heart of existing power relations and of which its protagonists obviously had a shrewd understanding.[8]

In conforming to these precepts, however subversively, feminists were aligning themselves, in one sense, with values associated with the middle classes. The element of philanthropy which surfaces in almost all their campaigns is apparent here too; some of the activity, at least, centred around the prostitution controversy and laid emphasis on the 'rescue' of 'fallen women'. The provision of homes and shelters for those working in prostitution might have provided invaluable accommodation, but it all too often aimed at moral 're-education', at curbing such a choice of livelihood. The philanthropic approach was only one minor aspect of such campaigns however and, despite their attachment to class-specific values, feminist agitators made explicit their class analysis. Prostitutes, for them, were largely compelled by poverty into servicing wealthy men who preached one morality and practised another, and though modern scholarship has suggested a rather different profile, we are concerned here with the contemporary feminist understanding of the problem.

It was marriage, however, which remained (even given the demographic trends we noted in Chapter 5) the common majority experience in women's lives. The very earliest of all feminist campaigns in our period were concerned with highlighting the inequalities within marriage – the loss of political status which a married woman exchanged for social status, the differing moral standards to which husbands and wives were expected to conform and their effect on the dissolution of failed marriages. At the start of our period, marriage for a woman demanded her yielding authority in concrete ways to her husband. Though most single women, more particularly in the wealthier brackets of society, would have been subject to paternal control, it was possible for them to administer their own affairs, to maintain a fair degree of economic independence and, if financially fortunate, to own property. On marriage, the legal assumption of coverture determined a woman's loss of all those rights. The eighteenth-century jurist, Blackstone, had laid down the fundamentals of this legal relationship.

By marriage, the husband and wife are one person in law: that is, the very being or legal existence of the woman is suspended during the marriage, or at least is incorporated and consolidated into that of the husband: under whose wing, protection, and cover, she performs everything.[9]

At marriage, both possession and control of a woman's property – including any monies she might earn from paid labour – passed to her husband unless property had been set up in trust for her under the law of equity. The option of land in trust was obviously a privilege accorded only to the wealthy, and in any case, such property, though legally the woman's possession, remained in a trustee's control. The husband's rights to property extended further into the human field too; the children of the marriage were his children and where a marriage was dissolved, custody was automatically ceded to the man.

As a legal minor, a married woman could neither sue nor be sued, nor enter into contracts, and her debts and legal wrangles were her husband's responsibility. At one level the injustice can be seen to affect both parties; a husband might suffer from his obligations towards a careless or free-spending partner. However, more importantly, that possible inconvenience was a direct consequence of the completeness of his power within the marriage. Women were disallowed any responsibility or competence within marriage. They were tied, moreover, by a moral standard to which their partners were not expected to adhere. In the few divorce cases heard in parliament prior to the marriage reform of the 1850s, few women came forward as petitioners. Where they did present cases involving adultery by their husbands, their bids for divorce were rejected, while adultery on the part of a wife would always be sufficient grounds for a husband's petition.[10]

Before 1857, when the new Divorce and Matrimonial Causes Act was passed, responsibility for divorce had been vested entirely in the hands of the church. Ecclesiastical law, of course, recognized very few grounds for divorce, and as the only other recourse was the obscure and costly one of a private petition to parliament, it remained a rare and restricted option. Only around two hundred such petitions were ever granted.[11] The 1857 act passed into the law with little seeming public activity. In part it was one of the measures by which the two conflicting legal systems of equity and common law were brought more closely into line with one another;[12] in part, it was a measure hurried through the Commons to head off the more alarming prospect of a proposed married women's property bill. The two issues were crucially linked; the substitution of the divorce legislation for that on property was seen as a placebo because the former contained a clause which gave a deserted wife the right to a protection order against her husband's attempting to possess her earnings or property thereafter. A husband's application in this instance could, however, revoke the wife's security. Both measures – divorce and property – were awarded a considerable degree of parliamentary attention in the 1850s, though they arrived there by different routes. Legislation affecting divorce arose principally out of a government-initiated Royal Commission on divorce instituted in 1850 whilst the less successful attempts to change the laws on married women's property arose directly out of feminist lobbying. As an early historian of the campaigns pointed out, 'There were now two women's Bills before the country, both dealing with that innermost sanctuary, the home, and to a certain extent they were used to destroy each other.'[13]

In 1854 Barbara Leigh Smith, one of the Langham Place circle of early feminists, had published her pamphlet attacking the legal position of married women. *A Brief Summary, in plain language, of the most important laws of England concerning Women, together with a few observations thereon* was the start of a campaign which was to become one of the most prominent, and indeed, successful of feminist agitations. By 1856, a petition bearing 3000 signatures and demanding a change in the law affecting married women's property was presented to both Houses of Parliament simultaneously with the organization of public meetings on the topic staged up and down the country. It is in this context that the rather hurried passing of the 1857 Divorce Act must be understood.

The 1857 act was an unsatisfactory one in feminist eyes, not only because it had been used as a political football which was to set back the cause of married women's property by more than a decade, nor simply because of the inadequacies of the provision for deserted wives. The act, in addition, enshrined the double sexual standard in the grounds it lay down as valid for securing divorce. The principal ground for divorce under the new legislation was adultery but though a husband could divorce his wife for adultery, the case was not as simple where he was the adulterer. Women's access to divorce was limited to cases where a husband's adultery was compounded by further sexual misdemeanours – what the Divorce Commissioners chose to call 'cases of aggravated enormity'.[14]

It shall be lawful for any Husband to present a Petition to the said Court, praying that his Marriage may be dissolved, on the Ground that his Wife has since the Celebration thereof been guilty of Adultery; and it shall be lawful for any Wife to present a petition to the said Court, praying that her Marriage may be dissolved, on the Ground that since the Celebration thereof her Husband has been guilty of incestuous Adultery, or of Bigamy with Adultery, or of Rape, or of Sodomy, or Bestiality, or of Adultery coupled with . . . Cruelty . . . or of Adultery coupled with Desertion, without reasonable Excuse, for Two Years or upwards.[15]

Much of the justification with which this inequality was thus legitimated centred again on the question of property and on the threat a wife's adultery might pose to inheritance and property transmission. A wife might not be permitted to *own* property but she was, of course, the vital link in maintaining the family.

The passing of the Divorce Act made divorce in limited instances at least a theoretical option for the misused wife, but even the small freedom thus won was in practice highly restricted.

A woman who sues for divorce must do so at her own expense. Now a married woman is never permitted to touch her own money, even if she has any – the man takes it all. If her fortune is in trust, the trustees always pay the annual interest to the husband. I would ask those best acquainted with such matters, whether a trustee is likely to supply monies to the wife for the purpose of suing for a divorce from her husband.[16]

Curiously, the major injustices wrought by the passing of the 1857 act were the subject of little feminist attention in the years immediately following. Concentration on other areas of reform – married women's property, education, the vote – overtook it in importance and it only surfaced again when organizations like the Women's Emancipation Union made divorce reform a plank of their policies in the early 1890s. The Clitheroe case of 1891 was also instrumental in re-opening the wider question of women's status within marriage. Mr and Mrs Jackson had lived apart throughout their brief marriage and when Jackson returned to Clitheroe from New Zealand, his wife had refused to live with him. After the failure of more orthodox methods of persuasion, he abducted her and held her captive while a legal suit was set in train. In the first instance, the judges upheld Jackson's right to imprison his wife for the restitution of his conjugal rights but the Court of Appeal overturned the judgement and set Mrs Jackson free. The couple none the less remained legally married.[17] Anomalies such as these, and more particularly where the freedom of the wife, physical or otherwise, was in question, became once more the subject of feminist agitation, revitalized by the growing articulacy of the social purity movement which stressed the immoralities consequent upon the double standard. In the preceding thirty years, however, the marriage debate centred far more crucially around the property issue.

The publication of Barbara Leigh Smith's influential *Brief Summary* had prompted the formation of the first married women's property committee in 1855. The failure of their legislative attempts in 1856–7 only further determined these activists and the campaign for legal change remained a prominent and central one for many years. The initial committee, based around Leigh Smith, her close friend Bessie Rayner Parkes and an older feminist, the Quaker Mary Howitt, included in time most of the leading activists of the day, both in London and elsewhere. Petitions to parliament from all around the country brought in other regional centres of feminist activity. Josephine Butler in Liverpool, Ursula Bright in Manchester, Elizabeth Wolstenholme in Cheshire, Harriet McIlquham in Cheltenham, all retained a long-term interest in the matter and figure in the subscription list of the committee even into the 1880s, as do London feminists such as Clementia Taylor, Frances Buss, Frances Power Cobbe and Lady Goldsmid. They were joined in the later years by a

younger generation of women. The focus of activity shifted at the
end of the 1860s from London to the north, where Ursula Mellor
Bright and Elizabeth Wolstenholme established a new married
women's property committee in Manchester. Wolstenholme was
its first secretary, and after her resignation in 1871 the post passed
to suffrage activist Lydia Becker.

It was an issue which raised interest across class barriers, more
particularly in relation to a husband's rights over his wife's earnings. Collections from working women's organizations feature in
the committee's subscriptions, and even in the earliest petition
scripted by Barbara Leigh Smith in 1855, those interests were not
neglected.

> . . . the sufferings thereupon ensuing, extend over all classes of
> society . . . if these laws often bear heavily upon women protected by
> the forethought of their relations, the social training of their husbands,
> and the refined customs of the rank to which they belong, how much
> more unequivocal is the injury sustained by women in the lower classes,
> for whom no such provisions can be made by their parents, who possess
> no means of appeal to extensive legal protection, and in regard to whom
> the education of the husband and the habits of his associates offer no
> moral guarantee for tender consideration of his wife.[18]

The question of the property of married women in this period,
perhaps far more obviously than any other issue, highlights the
friction between the public – property – and the private – love.
'In [men] it is called . . . "marrying money". If such marriages are
perpetrated for any love, it is plain of what the love must be!'[19]

In a sense, it was the recognition of this mixing of the spheres
which led women to their understanding of the concrete mechanisms of their subjugation, that the moral values of their society
were ascribed in accordance with sex. Moreover, it necessitated
tactics quite different to those employed in the spheres of women's
education or women's occupation. Relief could come only through
the official parliamentary channels, as with the suffrage issue, and
strategies therefore had to be aimed at convincing both politicians
and the public of the justice of female claims. The difference
between the moderate and polite conduct which characterizes the
married women's property campaign and the uncompromising
stance taken by those on the offensive against state regulation of
prostitution in the 1870s is a measure of the growing understanding
and confidence of feminist culture in this period. Many of the

same women were active in both areas – Josephine Butler, Emilie
Venturi, Elizabeth Wolstenholme (later Wolstenholme Elmy) –
but chose to temper their demands in accordance with the circum-
stantial tactics demanded.

The history of the property campaign is essentially a history on
the one hand of parliamentary manoeuvre, of bills and amendments throughout the late 1860s and 1870s, and on the other, of
hard propaganda and lobbying on the part of the women. Their
behaviour might have been less contentious on this issue than on
others, but their doggedness is unquestionable. Constant petitions
and memorials to parliament, articles in influential mainstream
journals, a careful monitoring of progress in the pages of the
feminist journals mark the stages of the campaign. When the first
and inadequate instalment of the Married Women's Property Act
finally won royal assent in 1870, the campaigners were not
mollified. It was 'vexatious, complicated, obscure in detail . . .
foolish and anomalous'.[20]

The women had every right to feel displeased with an act which
legal commentators subsequently dubbed 'a curiously tentative
and partial measure'.[21] As the women pointed out, the act which
parliament passed bore little relation to that for which they had
lobbied; Diana Worzala has suggested that the amendments made
to the bill before it became law were motivated by the threat that
if women were made totally financially independent, they might
leave their husbands![22]

The campaign was maintained throughout the 1870s with bills
and amendments to those bills coming before parliament in 1873,
1874, 1877, 1878, 1880 and 1881 before finally becoming law in
August 1882. The committee maintained the same range of
outlets – journals and tracts, parliamentary lobbying, public meetings – that they had utilized in the run-up to the first chapter.
Their success in maintaining a healthy subscription list is a clear
triumph, though in fact their total campaigning expenditure of
approximately £3200 was remarkably modest. The political focus
of the campaign, centring on parliamentary persuasion and
agitation, made this a far less financially ambitious project than
was undertaken in, for instance, the educational experiments
conducted under the feminist aegis.

The act of 1882 was widely regarded as a victory though the
women demurred that 'it is no triumph of women over men, but of
reason and justice over prejudice and selfishness'.[23] It effectively

equalized the rights and responsibilities of women irrespective of marital status, and with certain reservations was hailed as 'a step of profound importance' of which 'even thóse who have most actively worked for it . . . could scarcely have contemplated so triumphant a conclusion to their unceasing efforts'.[24] And at this juncture, their efforts did cease. The committee was, after all, a pressure group with a single and specific aim which it now felt had been met. Its members were all women prominent in other and now more pressing areas of feminist protest.

Some writers have argued that changes to the statutes governing marital relations in particular should be understood in a broader context of legal reform.[25] Mid-century judicial revision, undertaken to iron out some of the more startling and irksome absurdities which had passed into the law, was certainly an important element of the reforming spirit of these years. The two parallel legal systems of common law and equity on which court procedure was founded were often in opposition to one another, a contradiction which often resulted for the individual in costly legal wrangling. However, the issue of the property of married women, where the two systems were clearly at odds, had been the subject of vigorous lobbying for a considerable number of years before even the first instalment of reform was carried in 1870. In the context of the political manipulation and controversy surrounding its final victory, it is difficult to interpret it as merely the product of a general zeal for reform.

The campaign has a significance for us beyond the contestation of specifically defined rights. Many women cut their feminist teeth within this area of protest and through addressing the problems of property within marriage came to a clearer understanding of other aspects of female subjugation. Again, the yoking together of the divorce legislation of the 1850s and the struggles over married women's property brought home the point that the very structure of sexual and marital relations presupposed a double standard. When Frances Power Cobbe wrote her tract on married women's property in 1869, she concentrated on the moral dilemma.

That the legislative judgement of England should hold up before the world a perfect picture of what it understands that married life *ought* to be, is affirmed to be of much more consequence than that it should try to mend cases which must be bad at the best.[26]

And a decade earlier than the ever-shrewd Cobbe, Caroline Cornwallis had pointed out that between fathers and future husbands existing arrangements were unlikely to encourage a relationship of trust.

Indeed, so hazardous is it thought by fathers in general, to leave their daughter's property in the hands of the husband . . . that none who can afford to pay legal expenses, trust their property on so frail a foundation as the intended husband's prudence and integrity.[27]

The act of exposing one level of injustice within marriage inevitably led women directly to a questioning of countless similar discriminations. The issue of marriage occupied the crossover point between the need for parliamentary lobbying and the development of a fully-fledged moral critique of Victorian value systems.

The criticisms of marriage which feminists made arose, for the most part, not out of a disenchantment with the institution of marriage or intimate relations between men and women so much as through a dissatisfaction with the existing marital status quo. Criticisms of the feminist perspective, in the nineteenth century as much as today, all too frequently sank to a level of mud-slinging which characterized feminism as the voice of the bitter spinster. The feminist assault, however, was not on marriage, and indeed many looked forward to a time when the situation allowed real harmony and equality between the married couple. They did not seek, as critics constantly claimed, to undermine the practice or prevalence of marriage but to realign the rights of partners within that institution. Activists were evenly divided between married and single women, and a number of the women involved also brought their husbands into mixed committee work. It was Russell Gurney, husband of feminist Emilie Gurney, who piloted the first Married Women's Property Act successfully through its parliamentary voyage. Amelia Arnold, Clementia Taylor and Ursula Bright all brought their parliamentary husbands into the movement. They, along with Mrs Josephine Butler, Mrs Beddoe, Mrs Sophie Bryant, worked amicably with their unmarried colleagues – Emily Faithfull, Anna Swanwick, and Florence Davenport Hill.

Dissatisfaction with marital inequalities and the double standard did not rest with the issues of access to divorce and of separate property. The feminist onslaught was more thoroughgoing and their intrusion into the even more private area of husband–wife relations was important. The issue of marriage to a deceased wife's sister, pilloried in the comic operas of Gilbert and Sullivan as the 'annual blister' which parliament faced with monotonous regularity, and the rather grimmer phenomenon of assault within marriage were both areas of feminist debate, and frequently attracted the same core of campaigners.

Between 1882 and 1907, parliament pondered the morals of permitting or prohibiting the marriage of a widower to his sister-in-law in all but two of its sessions.[28] Back in the 1840s, parliamentary investigators had revealed that their willingness to regularize this particular relationship had as great a practical motive as it did a moral one.

The common foundation of such marriages is the familiar intercourse which necessarily prevails between a man and his sister-in-law, when, upon the death of a wife, she assumes her sister's place in the care of the children, and in the superintendence of the domestic establishment.[29]

The justification is a revealing one, for it exposes the class basis of the concern. The assumption of domestic duties by an unmarried sister would be a requirement only in households where there were no servants to perform such tasks. Women campaigners were fully alert to the partial nature of the proposed legislation.

The deceased Wife's Sister's Bill instead of dealing broadly and clearly with the question simply proposes to legalise one special and privileged class of such marriages, that of a man with his dead wife's sister, leaving all other marriages of affinity illegal and their offspring illegitimate . . . the promoters of the Bill have explicitly and repeatedly refused to enlarge its scope declaring that they would rather throw over the bill than legalise the marriage of a woman with her dead husband's brother.[30]

The historian of this legislative measure has asserted that the feminist movement showed little interest in the question, and though it was certainly never adopted as a major campaigning battle, feminists were none the less conscious of it as yet another retrenchment of the double standard.[31] The *Women's Suffrage Journal* called it 'a new and glaring inequality between the sexes in the matter of marriage'.[32]

Of far more central concern from the 1870s was a growing

awareness of and anxiety over violence within marriage. It is difficult to say with any authority whether marital assault was on the increase as was supposed at this juncture; more important is the perception at the time that it was a growing problem. Legal opinion certainly did little to prohibit male violence. 'The husband . . . might give his wife moderate correction . . . by domestic chastisement, in the same moderation that a man is allowed to correct his apprentices or children.'[33] And as Frances Power Cobbe pointed out, it was a facet of human suffering which was not taken seriously. 'The proceeding seems to be surrounded by a certain halo of jocosity which inclines people to smile whenever they hear of a case of it.'[34]

Cobbe's important denunciation of wife-abuse, an act she saw as resulting in large part from the degrading pressure of poverty, re-opened the marriage debate in the late 1870s. Her assertion that the new divorce court remained an option beyond the reach of poor women, whom she felt to be more at risk, prompted an evaluation of the option of separation. In effect, what the passing of the 1878 Matrimonial Causes Act brought into existence was a class apartheid; wealthier women might obtain full divorces via the workings of the 1857 act, albeit on a limited number of grounds, while working-class women were offered the cheaper but more restricted alternative of a separation order granted through a magistrate's court, which, of course, prohibited the option of re-marriage. Cobbe saw the new measure as a means of empowering wives, in giving them the means whereby they could break the cycle of violence, but her suggestions had been, as one might imagine, considerably more far-reaching than those actually implemented under the 1878 legislation. Cobbe argued that the right of separation should be amplified by automatic maternal custody of children and by maintenance orders for a wife and her children against the offending husband.[35] The subsequent history of these changes shows that the option of separation was utilized principally by aggrieved women while divorce remained primarily a vehicle for male use.[36]

Before and after the passing of the 1878 act, feminists were concerned with male violence against women and their publications kept a close watch on legal proceedings in this area. The furore over the Clitheroe case in 1891 was by no means unique; the use of force to compel women to their conjugal duties – or occasionally to prevent a forbidden union – was a familiar story.

The report in the *Women's Suffrage Journal* in 1875 of a husband threatening a recalcitrant wife and of the magistrates rejecting her suit against him was a common enough event; some twenty years earlier, Caroline Cornwallis had cited another similar case – that of Mrs Cochrane – in her *Westminster Review* piece on married women's property.

Property, of course, was fundamental to this as to other aspects of the marriage question. In her important article, Cobbe made the direct connection between ownership and the reality of violence with stark effect.

The notion that a man's wife is his PROPERTY, in the sense in which a horse is his property . . . is the fatal root of incalculable evil and misery. . . . It is even sometimes pleaded on behalf of poor men, that they possess *nothing else* but their wives, and that, consequently, it seems doubly hard to meddle with the exercise of their power in that narrow sphere.[37]

Even the question of property, however, was fraught with difficulties for the married woman. On the one hand, men's rights extended over children as much as wives, another crucial site for feminist protest during this period and culminating in 1886 in the Guardianship of Infants Act. This measure finally secured legal admissibility for a mother's wishes though the husband's authority was only marginally diminished. On the other hand, where maintenance was the issue at stake, the law was rather less fastidious about asserting men's sway over their wives and families. The financial problem was most acute in cases of illegitimate offspring, and many feminists believed that the bastardy clauses introduced under the new Poor Law of 1834 and effective into the 1870s were another means of sanctioning and protecting male vice. Effectively, the new welfare provisions of 1834 made mothers almost wholly responsible for the support of their bastard children, a measure which sat in curious contradiction to the legal power fathers exercised over their offspring.[38] The careless drafting of the 1872 Bastardy Law Amendment Act such that mothers had no legal redress against the fathers of children born before the passing of the act once more catalysed feminist action. The indefatigible Elizabeth Wolstenholme not only sought to have the defective law amended put proffered remedies to women trapped by it.[39]

Illegitimacy, of course, highlights a moral arena we have not yet discussed. There was concern in Victorian England over the levels of illegitimacy, a phenomenon more significant in rural than in urban areas.[40] In the urban context, far more anxiety was voiced over a perceived increase in the incidence of prostitution and, as its corollary, of venereal disease. The whole issue of prostitution was regarded with gravity by the Victorian establishment but attention was focused principally by the energetic activities of feminists, on the operation of the Contagious Diseases Acts from the late 1860s on.

The CD acts, as they were known, were prompted by the high incidence of venereal disease in the British armed forces; 29 per cent of all army men admitted to hospital in 1862 and 12.5 per cent of naval hospital admissions in the same year were for treatment of sexually transmitted diseases.[41] Attempts to subject enlisted men to periodic genital examination met with considerable rank-and-file resistance and government turned instead to the regulation of the women with whom soldiers and sailors consorted. The acts, which were applicable in eighteen named garrison towns and ports such as Plymouth, Colchester, Chatham and Woolwich, allowed police to apprehend women suspected of being what the acts dubbed a 'common prostitute' and of harbouring a contagious disease. Though successive acts changed the form of the legislation slightly, any such woman was required to attend upon a genital medical examination to ascertain whether she was, in fact, infectious. Where examination proved positive, she could be detained for a period of up to three months to effect a treatment. A woman's refusal to co-operate with what was effectively a suspension of *habeas corpus* could lead to a prison sentence of one month, doubling in duration for any subsequent recalcitrance. In apprehending a 'common prostitute', the police relied on certain indicators of guilt, viz: 'residence in a brothel; solicitation in the streets; frequenting places where prostitutes resort; being informed against by soldiers and sailors; and lastly, the admission of the woman herself'.[42] The first of the acts was set in motion in 1864 and a second measure extended its operation in 1866 and again in 1869. By that time, organized opposition to the acts was gaining ground and by the end of 1869 a Ladies' National Association for the Repeal of the Contagious Diseases Acts (LNA) had been founded.

Few feminists were not, at the very least, tacit supporters of the LNA's work and many familiar names were appended to its first petition. The list reads like the subscription list of the married women's property committee: Josephine Butler, Ursula Bright, Lydia Becker, Clementia Taylor, Elizabeth Wolstenholme, Emilie Venturi. The criticisms they made of the acts were thorough and wide-ranging, dealing as centrally with the issues of class and poverty as with gender. Crucially, their weapon was the blatant double standard which the acts' proponents rehearsed time and time again. The repealers were well-organized and effectively vocal. *The Shield*, a weekly circular giving news of the acts and of protests against them, began publication in March 1870. Its first issue spelt out succinctly the varied grounds of the objections.

These Acts of Parliament deprive all women resident in the districts to which they apply of all safeguards of personal liberty and unblemished character; they subject those submitted to their operation to indecent outrage or cruel imprisonment; they lend the protection of the law to sin, aiming exclusively and professedly at rendering safe indulgence in vicious pleasures; and they tax the virtuous and the hardworking for this immoral purpose.

The various grounds of the attack are interesting. Repeal organizations exhibited a mixture of strong feminist outrage over the double standard, an adherence to the principles of individual liberty of person, a humanitarian concern with the subjected women and a shrewd nod in the direction of the shocked taxpayer. Just as feminist activists dominated the organizational channels of the campaign, so did the feminist reading of the acts outweigh the other concerns of repealers. When Josephine Butler gave evidence in March 1871 before the Royal Commission on the acts on behalf of her LNA, her analysis of their motive and their effect was clear and unequivocal.

We claim that laws shall not be made whose practical effect, so far as they are successful at all, is to offer protection and immunity to the sinner in the practice of his sin. . . . Neither can our moral objections to these Acts be met by the assurances that a certain number of women are reclaimed under their operations. I ask where are the men reclaimed by them? . . . Prove to us, if you can, that these Acts promote chastity among men, for that is what we are concerned about.[43]

Butler's aim was perfect; while feminists and their supporters condemned the acts as a means of sanctioning the use of prostitutes by 'providing healthy women for profligate men',[44] the CD Commission continued to assert ineffectually the moral basis of the legislation.

The Committee would have more hesitation in so earnestly recommending a periodical examination of the public prostitutes under the Act, and their seclusion until cured, did they not confidently feel that in so doing they are acting not only in the interests of the community, but especially so in that of the women themselves . . . and, were they not, moreover, convinced that such examination in nowise involves the legalisation or, in any respect, the encouragement, of vice.[45]

The 'deep sympathy'[46] they professed to feel for the women affected by the acts did not, however, extend to their assessment of the acts' effects on them.

The case of a modest woman submitting her person to a medical examination by a private practitioner, and that of a prostitute coming up every fortnight to be examined by a medical officer, are very different.[47]

Indeed, the language chosen by the architects of the legislation reveals some significant ideas about their placing of the public and the private. They had no compunction in exposing women to this erosion of personal liberty, for they assumed pre-eminently that the affected women were not ladies. Their use of the term 'public women' to describe women engaged in the commerce of prostitution is revealing; such women had transgressed the acceptable boundaries of femininity and had thus placed themselves outside the grace of male protection. Their resort to sex as a means of livelihood was a double transgression: they had penetrated the male world of public work and had brought private behaviour into that public context in doing so. It was left to feminist analysts to make the connections between women's choices and economic necessity. Elizabeth Wolstenholme Elmy (formerly Elizabeth Wolstenholme) talked of 'women who are driven to this unhappy life in most cases by sheer poverty', while one of the many regular repeal publications denounced the acts as 'a piece of CLASS LEGISLATION. . . . Ladies who ride in their carriages through the streets at night are in no danger of being molested. But what about working women?'[48]

The recognition by feminists that class was an important

consideration won them the support of working men fearing the effects of the acts on their own wives and daughters. In her statements to the 1871 Commissioners, Butler referred to the common ground of dissatisfaction that feminists and working people alike shared. 'Whereas all legislation hitherto . . . has been directed against the poor only, we insist, and the working men insist, that it shall also apply to the rich profligate.'[49] Organized agitation for repeal was thus not wholly confined to feminists, though the prominent figures in the LNA which spearheaded the campaign were certainly associated with the women's movement. Judith Walkowitz has stressed that many LNA women came from a background of similar, if less explicitly sexual, moral reform campaigns, anti-slavery and temperance in particular.[50] In the feminist context, CD agitation proved important in crystallizing the value of a wider feminist analysis. In the wake of the suspension in 1883 and final abandonment of the acts in 1886, many women chose to concentrate not on older-style concrete feminist campaigns such as the founding of schools or agitating for entry into the professions, but on obtaining a single moral standard for men and women alike.

Social purity organizations dedicated to erasing the double standard proliferated and though not all were feminist-inspired or peopled, their common aim was the eradication of what they regarded as male vice. The Social Purity League, the Moral Reform Union and a host of similarly inclined organizations effectively continued to broadcast the opinions first openly formulated through the LNA though in slightly different channels. According to Sheila Jeffreys, the social purity movement of the 1880s was interested primarily in eliminating prostitution and female child sexual abuse, and concentrated thus on women's victimization.[51]

Looking back on a lifetime of committed feminism, Millicent Garrett Fawcett saw four aspects to 'a many-sided movement . . . (1) education, (2) an equal moral standard between men and women, (3) professional and industrial liberty, and (4) political status'.[52] These were sentiments that differed little in essence from those of Josephine Butler some quarter of a century earlier when she maintained that, 'we felt that it was necessary, while combating the State Regulation of vice . . . also to work against all those disabilities and injustices which affect the interests of women.'[53]

There had been recognition earlier within the feminist movement that the moral issue was coterminous with more practical political concerns; the process of awareness begun with marital legislation was consolidated in the course of the CD repeal agitation and found expression in the last two decades of the century alike in social purity crusades and in an increased feminist commitment to temperance. The rise in women's involvement in the temperance movement from the 1870s coincides with the beginnings of feminist agitation around moral issues.[54] The connection between drink and violence was one of the chief worries. ' . . . what are the principal incitements to such outbursts of savage fury among the classes wherein Wife-beating prevails[?] . . . The first is undoubtedly *Drink*.'[55] Alcoholism led not only to violence, of course, but to other forms of family disruption which signalled the moral dissolution so feared in Victorian England. A drinking husband would be likely to expend those wages which would otherwise represent the family budget on his habit, and it was also assumed that both alcohol and the venues in which it was consumed were part of a chain of moral slippage leading its victims to further misconducts. 'Prohibitionism is a noteworthy example of that alliance between feminism and middle class puritanism which Bernard Shaw so detested.'[56]

Neither the Edwardian playwright quoted here nor the author of that passage, Brian Harrison, quite see the power and significance of that alliance. The 'puritanism' feminists exhibited was a political analysis of the workings of a double standard which ruled their lives with considerable force. The more liberal option of relaxing moral values would have involved sanctioning a continuum of repression under the guise of liberation. 'The woman's task is indeed hard and discouraging when all her efforts fail to prevent the imposition of fresh disabilities, and when she herself so clearly sees what is wanted to prevent the forging of new chains.'[57]

We may thus begin to understand the absence of a feminist input into the struggles to legitimize contraceptive practice which were occurring roughly at the same time as the emergence of this alternative feminist morality. It is interesting to note, in this context, that the Malthusian League, a body devoted to spreading the doctrine of family limitation, had supported the LNA's repeal campaign despite their differences on the contraception issue. We might today see contraception as fundamental to a woman's own control of her body, but one might as easily see the inescapability from male sexual attention which it could also imply. In a climate of opinion which denied an active female sexuality, control of reproduction could, in fact, spell further exploitation. In championing its spread, women would be sanctioning and licensing the male sexuality which they felt to be responsible for their position. Their stand against a free sexuality was, in fact, a protest against prostitution and pornography, against the 'shameful and immoral inequality and injustice, as between husband and wife, of the English Law of Divorce',[58] against their exclusion from the initial means of altering these injustices – the political arena. Centrally, women were attacking the rights of male privilege by denying *all* its values. It was their understanding of the connections between this and other spheres of women's protests which distinguishes them from other moral reformers and suffuses the single issue campaigns in which they were often active with a consistent feminist awareness. Mrs John Beddoe, an associate of Mary Carpenter and a suffrage worker, underlined 'the unspeakable importance of adding to our claims for just *Rights* of all kinds, the adoption of the highest standards of *Duty*.'[59]

In their creation of a female-defined and alternative morality, women were not retreating into the private world, but they were maintaining staunchly some measure of a separate sphere reasoning. Their pride and identity as feminists was consciously based on sexual difference; the political equality they sought was not based on a desire to emulate men but to balance existing male opinion with women's views. It is interesting to note, in this context, that feminist analysis was not wholly confined to the specifics of *women's* grievances in this period but encompassed a broader moral critique. Many activists were involved in the strong anti-vivisection movement of the day and the grounds of their condemnation of the practice is illuminating.

The sole element in Existence is force. . . . Consisting of force only, intellectual or physical, humanity is fully represented by the man. The woman, and the qualities represented in her, being affectional only . . . are unreal, superfluous, detrimental, and ought to be suppressed. The head is all, the heart is nothing; intellect is all, character or disposition nothing; consequences are all; means nothing.[60]

The marked interest in the moral sphere which grew to such significant proportions towards the end of the century was a double-headed beast; in part, it was a logical successor to early moral reform campaigns bringing into feminism women who had championed more immediate rights, but it also gave those women a means of understanding those grievances through the lens of gender. There was a clear intellectual difference between concern over the immorality of prostitutes and of prostitution, and that measured the distance they had travelled from the authoritarianism of philanthropy to the qualified libertarianism of feminism. The rescue of fallen women did not necessarily cast attention on their clients or on the sexual system in which client and whore were enmeshed whereas the evaluation of the institution, highlighted by CD repeal agitation, forced the issue.

Olive Banks, as well as Linda Gordon and Ellen DuBois in the American context, have suggested that this tendency in fact represented a move towards a greater conservatism within the women's movement, while Richard Evans sees it as effecting a sharp radicalization, as women took on a host of powerful male organizations; the brewers, the police, the doctors.[61] In one sense, the feminist perspective was turning inwards to an acceptance of separate spheres.

Women's *external* position . . . is still one of entire subjection. . . . But if we look more closely, we find her armed with a power which man can neither cast off nor abridge, for it springs from her natural position towards him, which cannot be altered whatever be the outward forms of society.[62]

Out of that appreciation, however, came the strength and the ability to challenge publicly issues confined either to a private morality or to the male world, and thus hitherto closed to women. 'Private morality could be applied to the public level.'[63] By embracing the ideological stance which made the private sphere their domain and intentionally challenging it in the public sphere, feminists effectively highlighted the moral contradictions inherent in their society. We may today regard their stand as a fundamentally conservative one, but it gave them at the time a remarkable freedom and power; through containment and confinement women could do more than campaign around specific issues. Women, in effect, offered an alternative morality inherently critical of the ideology in which they claimed belief.

Notes and references

1 Leonore Davidoff and Catherine Hall, 'The Architecture of Public and Private Life. English Middle-Class Society in a Provincial Town 1780–1850', in Derek Fraser and Anthony Sutcliffe (eds), *The Pursuit of Urban History* (London, 1983), pp. 327–45 (p. 344).

2 Ben Barker-Benfield, 'The Spermatic Economy: A Nineteenth-Century View of Sexuality', *Feminist Studies*, **1** (1972) 1, pp. 45–74 (p. 58); see also the work of Jeffrey Weeks and in particular his *Sexuality and Its Discontents. Meanings, Myths and Modern Sexualities* (London, 1985), and Michel Foucault, *The History of Sexuality*, Vol. 1 (Harmondsworth, 1981).

3 Martha Vicinus, 'Sexuality and Power: A Review of Current Work in the History of Sexuality', *Feminist Studies*, **8** (1982) 1, pp. 133–56 (p. 135).

4 Linda Gordon and Ellen DuBois, 'Seeking Ecstasy on the Battlefield: Danger and Pleasure in Nineteenth Century Feminist Sexual Thought', *Feminist Review*, **13** (February 1983), pp. 42–54; Judith R. Walkowitz, 'Jack the Ripper and the Myth of Male Violence', *Feminist Studies*, **8** (1982) 3, pp. 542–74 (p. 563).

5 Walkowitz, 'Jack the Ripper', p. 567.

6 Frances Power Cobbe, 'Wife-Torture in England', *Contemporary Review* (1878), pp. 55–87 (p. 81).

7 Ethel Snowden, *The Feminist Movement* (London, 1911), p. 114.

8 Alex Tyrrell, ' "Woman's Mission" and Pressure Group Politics in Britain (1825–60)', *Bulletin of the John Rylands University Library of Manchester* **63** (1980) 1, pp. 194–230 (p. 220).

9 Quoted in K. O'Donovan, 'The Male Appendage – Legal Definitions of Women', in S. Burman (ed.), *Fit Work for Women* (London, 1979), pp. 134–52 (p. 136).

10 Keith Thomas, 'The Double Standard', *Journal of the History of Ideas* **XX** (1959) 2, pp. 195–216 (pp. 199–202).

11 Thomas, 'The Double Standard', p. 201.

12 Iris Minor, 'Working-Class Women and Matrimonial Law Reform, 1890–1914', in D. E. Martin and D. Rubinstein (eds), *Ideology and the Labour Movement. Essays Presented to John Saville* (London, 1979), pp. 103–24 (p. 104).

13 Ray Strachey, *The Cause. A Short History of the Women's Movement in Great Britain* (London, 1978), p. 74.

14 Parliamentary Papers, House of Commons, 1852–3 [1604] xl, *First Report of the Commissioners appointed to enquire into the Law of Divorce*, p. 22.

15 20 & 21 Vic. c.85. An Act to amend the Law relating to Divorce and Matrimonial Causes in England, 28 August 1857.

16 Harriet Grote, 'The Law of Marriage', in *Collected Papers in Prose and Verse 1842–62* (London, 1862), p. 284.

17 A very clear account of the case will be found in Chapter 5 of David Rubinstein's *Before the Suffragettes. Women's Emancipation in the 1890s* (Sussex, 1896).

18 Quoted in Hester Burton, *Barbara Bodichon* (London, 1949), p. 70.

19 Thodosia Marshall, 'Love and Money', *Kettledrum* (June, 1869) pp. 355–9 (p. 356).

20 *Fourth Annual Report of the Married Women's Property Committee*, 22 September 1871, pp. 3; 4.

21 Montague Lush, 'Changes in the Law Affecting the Rights, Status and Liabilities of Married Women', in *A Century of Law Reform. Twelve Lectures on the Changes in the Law of England during the nineteenth century* (London, 1901), pp. 342–78 (p. 353).

22 Diana Mary Chase Worzala, 'The Langham Place Circle: The Beginnings of the Organised Women's Movement in England, 1854–70'. Unpublished PhD thesis, University of Wisconsin-Madison, 1982, p. 450.

23 *Final Report of the Married Women's Property Committee*, 1882, p. 54.

24 *Women's Union Journal*, **80** (September 1882), VII.

25 See in particular, Lee Holcombe, 'Victorian Wives and Property: Reform of the Married Women's Property Law, 1857–1882', in Martha Vicinus (ed.), *A Widening Sphere. Changing Roles of Victorian Women* (London, 1980), pp. 3–28 (p. 4).

26 Frances Power Cobbe, *Criminals, Idiots, Women and Minors. Is the classification sound? A Discussion on the Laws concerning the property of married women* (Manchester, 1869), p. 8.

27 [Caroline Frances Cornwallis], 'The Property of Married Women', *Westminster Review* **66** (October, 1856), pp. 331–60 (pp. 344–5).

28 Cynthia Fansler Behrman, 'The Annual Blister: A Sidelight on Victorian Social and Parliamentary History,' *Victorian Studies*, **XI** (1968), 4, pp. 483–502 (p. 483).

29 PP, House of Commons, 1847–8 [973] xxviii. *First Report of the Commissioners appointed to inquire into the state and operation of the Law of Marriage*, p. x.

30 British Library, Additional Manuscript 47450, f. 230, Elizabeth Wolstenholme Elmy to Harriet McIlquham, 26 November 1895.

31 Cynthia Behrman, 'The Annual Blister', p. 494.

32 *Women's Suffrage Journal*, **II** (March 1871), 12, pp. 22–3.

33 Quoted in Montague Lush, pp. 345–6.

34 Frances Power Cobbe, 'Wife-Torture', pp. 56–7.

35 Frances Power Cobbe, 'Wife-Torture', p. 82.

36 Gail L. Savage, 'The Operation of the 1857 Divorce Act, 1860–
    1910. A Research Note', *Journal of Social History* 16 (Summer
    1983) 4, pp. 103–10 (p. 105).

37 Frances Power Cobbe, 'Wife-Torture', pp. 62–3.

38 Ursula Henriques, 'Bastardy and the New Poor Law', *Past and
    Present*, 37 (1967), pp. 103–29.

39 *Women's Suffrage Journal* 111 (2 September 1872), 31, p. 123.

40 Albert Leffingwell, *Illegitimacy and the Influence of the Seasons
    upon Conduct. Two Studies in Demography* (London/New York,
    1892). John Andrew Blaikie suggested this source to me.

41 PP, House of Commons, 1867–8 [4031] xxxvii, *Report of the
    Committee appointed to enquire into the Pathology and Treatment
    of the Venereal Diseases.*

42 PP, House of Commons, 1871, C.408, xix, *Report of the Royal
    Commission upon the Administration and Operation of the
    Contagious Diseases Acts*, p. 6.

43 PP, House of Commons, 1871, C.408, xix, *Minutes of Evidence*,
    p. 438.

44 *The Storm-Bell* (January 1898), p. 2.

45 PP, House of Commons, 1867–8 [4031] xxxvii, p. xxx.

46 PP, House of Commons, 1867–8 [4031] xxxvii, p. xxx.

47 PP, House of Commons, 1871, C.408, xix, p. 14.

48 British Library, Add. MS. 47451, f. 99, Elizabeth Wolstenholme
    Elmy to Harriet McIlquham, 20 May 1897; *The Storm-Bell*
    (January 1898) p. 3.

49 PP, House of Commons, 1871, C.408, xix, p. 439.

50 Judith R. Walkowitz, *Prostitution and Victorian Society. Women,
    class and the state* (Cambridge, 1980), p. 123.

51 Sheila Jeffreys, *The Spinster and her Enemies. Feminism and
    Sexuality 1880–1930* (London, 1985), p. 6.

52 Millicent Garrett Fawcett, *What I Remember* (London, 1924),
    p. 117.

53 Josephine E. Butler, *Personal Reminiscences of A Great Crusade*
    (London, 1896), p. 83.

54 Ruth Bordin, *Woman and Temperance. The Quest for Power and
    Liberty, 1873–1900* (Philadelphia, 1981), p. 159.

55 Frances Power Cobbe, 'Wife-Torture', p. 65.

56 Brian Harrison, 'The British Prohibitionists, 1853–1872. A
    Biographical Analysis', *International Review of Social History*, XV
    (1970) 3, pp. 375–467 (p. 402).

57 Mary Ashton Dilke, *Women's Suffrage* (London, 1885), p. 55.

58 Women's Emancipation Union, *Second Report*, 13 March 1894,
    p. 1.

59 Quoted in Frances Power Cobbe, *Life of Frances Power Cobbe By Herself* (London, 1894), II, 233.

60 *'The Woman' and the Age: A Letter Addressed to the Rt. Hon. W. E. Gladstone, MP* (London, 1881), p. 12.

61 Olive Banks, *Faces of Feminism. A Study of Feminism as a Social Movement* (Oxford, 1981), pp. 84–5; R. J. Evans, *The Feminists. Women's Emancipation Movements in Europe, America and Australasia 1840–1920* (London, 1977), p. 36.

62 Maria G. Grey and Emily Shirreff, *Thoughts on Self-Culture Addressed to Women* (London, 1872), p. 2.

63 Jean Bethke Elshtain, *Public Man, Private Woman* (Princeton, 1981), p. 238.

Chronology

1857 Divorce and Matrimonial Causes Act passed.

1861 Abolition of death penalty for sodomy.

1864 Contagious Diseases Act passed.

1866 Contagious Diseases Act passed.

1869 Ladies' National Association for the Repeal of the Contagious Diseases Acts formed.

1872 Bastardy Law Amendment Act passed.

1873 Social Purity Alliance founded (by men).

1878 Matrimonial Causes Act passed.

1879 Association for the Improvement of Public Morals founded.

1881 Moral Reform Union founded.

1884 Matrimonial Causes Act passed.

1885 Criminal Law Amendment Act passed.
Scandal over W. T. Stead and 'Maiden Tribute' affair.

1886 Guardianship of Infants Act passed.
Maintenance of Wives Act passed.
Contagious Diseases Acts repealed.

1889 Incest Bill.

1891 Clitheroe case, *Regina v. Jackson*.

1895 Matrimonial Causes Act passed.

7 Epilogue

Writing in 1911, Ethel Snowden called Britain 'the present storm-centre of the world's feminist movement'.[1] The previous half century had seen massive though by no means conclusive strides forward for women effected through their own efforts.

One after the other the citadels of education, science, art, social service, politics were all attacked and one after the other – with the exception of the last – the portals of these jealously guarded male monopolies were grudgingly opened.[2]

The early twentieth century saw some decisive shifts in the women's movement. The few years of political clamour surrounding the militant suffragettes from around 1908 until the cessation of their activities on the outbreak of war in 1914 has served to mask effectively not only the alternative feminist tactics of that same period but also the vast range of activity preceding it in the later nineteenth century. This historical distortion which rendered all women's struggles other than that of the suffragettes either invisible or dully insignificant has been a major factor in focusing our historical definition of feminism on the fight for the vote. Even within the period in which the franchise issue climaxed into physical struggle, other feminist issues remained important within the movement. Their eclipse has both narrowed and starved our understanding.

One hears people talk sometimes as if the suffrage movement *were* the women's movement, and as if, when the vote shall be won, there will be no more women's movement. . . . Shall the vote be at once the record of the progress of women and its grave?[3]

Written in 1914, this heartfelt protest shows that this process of stripping the movement of long-term or broadly conceived significance is no new phenomenon. Neither in the Edwardian nor the Victorian period, as we have seen, was the parliamentary vote the sole definitive feature of feminist thinking or action. Many of the key issues first recognized in the nineteenth century remained at least partially unresolved – equal pay, equal rights to divorce, access to a host of closed professions including the law – and the moral issues which had become so dominant in the closing years of the previous century all remained prominent. The National Vigilance Association and the Association for Moral and Social Hygiene took up the same sorts of issues in the early years of the new century as those which had taxed Josephine Butler and her associates in the 1880s – new amendments to the Criminal Law Amendment Act of 1885, punishment for incest, the problem of prostitution.[4] Cicely Hamilton's polemic of 1909, *Marriage As A Trade*, spelt out the implications for women of marriage, while four years later Christabel Pankhurst published her tirade against the prevalence of VD in men, *The Great Scourge*. Clearly, these were issues of some prominence for feminists during precisely that period when the vote is said to have overridden all other interests. The vote was never, then, the consuming issue that historians and others both at the time and since have judged it to be, and indeed one recent reappraisal of the significance of the physicality that came to mark suffragette activity emphasizes the legacy which the struggle for the vote owed to the social purity debates of the late nineteenth century. The bodily sacrifice made so public by militant feminists, from street-level physical assault to the hunger strike, psychologically and politically symbolized the bodily sacrifice to men which was women's perpetual history and which had been the underlying theme of the social purity campaigners.[5] Their arrests and prison ordeals exaggerated the gap between, on the one hand, their strength in enduring the assaults of the state as well as of individual men, and on the other, their female role as victims of men and of male violence in all its forms.

The accent on suffragette activity has also masked the growing politicization of working-class women in the Edwardian period, both within growing socialist organizations and the trade union movement, and in more specifically feminist campaigns. They were torn often between class solidarity and gender solidarity. The growing gulf between the new labour organizations and the feminists over the relative urgency of full adult male suffrage or partial women's suffrage epitomizes a problem which had surfaced only marginally in the nineteenth century but which was to become central as the working-class voice grew stronger, and as partial measures of reform raised alike the hopes of unrepresented men and women.

The Edwardian period necessarily signalled different conditions and different priorities than those which had absorbed the energies of earlier generations of feminists. They had none the less established a powerful and wide-ranging movement which enjoyed considerable success in winning its demands and, perhaps more importantly, had articulated a new and positive consciousness of commonalty among women, strengthened by the networks which offered not simply a guaranteed core of committed workers for the cause but, crucially, a sense of human contact at all levels.

Despite the dilution which the urgency of their legislative needs forced upon nineteenth-century feminists – a compromise which the suffragettes in the 1910s saw as no longer tenable – they had made decisive and far-reaching attempts to acquire a new set of political codes, of language and behaviour. If we must measure movements in terms of their successes or failures (though their significance may, and often does, lie entirely elsewhere) we should point to these factors as much as to the passing of the married women's property acts or the establishment of women's colleges at Oxford and Cambridge.

It is true, too, that in that time, women failed to capture the parliamentary vote. It was to be 1923 before equal rules were to apply for both sexes in cases of divorce. Employers continued to impose a marriage bar as well as a lower wage scale well into the twentieth century (and even today). But we must still be wary of determining success only in the context of public or parliamentary achievement. Against all odds, the women's movement of the later nineteenth century not only sustained itself and grew in numbers and strength throughout this period, but most importantly developed through its struggles an understanding of the politics of sexual disability and a recognition of women's collective interests. In many instances women remained active in the movement even through the trauma of personal tragedy. One thinks of Elizabeth Garrett Anderson losing her second child from meningitis in 1875 (and indeed, maintaining not only her political commitments but her medical career even after marriage) or of the bitter personal blow which Garrett's elevation to the post of Dean at the London School of Medicine for Women spelt for her co-worker Sophia Jex-Blake. Emilie Dilke faced scorn and suspicion in the mid 1880s when her second husband's political career was destroyed by a highly public and somewhat scurrilous adultery scandal. It would not be unfair to surmise that many women gained strength and comfort from the close networks which embraced and supported them within the feminist movement.

It was a movement which succeeded in largely rejecting the partisan character of existing politics. 'Women of conservative mould are allied with those of radical temperament in the British women's movement.'[6] Autonomy, at every level, was its definitive feature: autonomy from existing political divisions, autonomy from male inteference, autonomy in separate campaigns. Its need to promote a collective identity based on gender was well served by such a tactic; the difference of sex made it crucial for the movement to sever relations with a male-identified world. There was no retreat, but a positive, critical and fundamentally separate stand. As Constance Maynard said uncompromisingly. 'The great fact stands clear in past history that collective man has abused his power to so terrible an extent that the utmost indignation is stirred by our sight of what has happened, and is still happening.'[7]

The relationship between personal and political liberty was of fundamental importance for women whatever their class backgrounds. Helena Swanwick remarked rather tartly and with biting accuracy that,

Women are notoriously the poor sex. Even a woman who figures as a rich woman is often merely an *article de luxe* for the man who provides for her, and though he may hang her neck with jewels, he does not readily give her a cheque for her suffrage society.[8]

We can trace the tightrope that women invariably walked not only through contemporary eyes but historiographically, and see too how easy it is for historians to fall into the trap of distortion, rendering women passive objects on whom reforms and emancipations were visited rather than as autonomous and active agents of that change. The tendency is, as one might expect, more marked where working women are the subject of discussion. In his appraisal of the changing position of women, Richard Titmuss ascribes the reduction in childbearing in the early years of this century to the father rather than the mother.

This . . . can only have been exercised with the consent – if not the approval – of the husband. . . . We are thus led to interpret this development as a desired change within the working-class family rather than as a revolt by women against the authority of men on the analogy of the campaign for political emancipation.[9]

The separation Titmuss draws between changes in family size and women's political freedoms is erroneous, though understandable in the context in which he was writing, where the divorce between the public and the private has remained in force. In 1896, Elizabeth Wolstenholme Elmy had remarked to her friend Harriet McIlquham, 'the only absolute right I should claim for a woman over a man is that she should never be made a mother against her will'.[10] For feminists both in the nineteenth century and today, healing that split has been one of the most fundamental and widely recognized precepts by which the movement can be defined. From the early dissatisfaction among feminists over the terms on which the 1857 Divorce and Matrimonial Causes Act was passed onwards, women had protested the need to see their personal situations in the political context of male rule. Even where they absented themselves, as many did in their writings, from having suffered personally the abuse of men, they fully acknowledged its frequency and its significance in understanding women's oppression.

This unconventional view of politics, though now current again within today's feminist circles, has perhaps obscured feminist thinking for historians more accustomed to severely hierarchical and policy-based political organizations. The sheer breadth of concerns with which the women's movement busied itself in this period and its conscious rejection of an overall formal organizing principle stand out as the characteristics of nineteenth-century feminism, at least in England.

European and American feminism differed in many respects, and the English example certainly does not serve as a cross-cultural model. The American situation was heightened by the active anti-slavery movement as well as the specific politics laid down under the country's Constitution. In Europe, where industrial advances came at a later date than in Britain and where a largely rural economy was often more significant, things were again different. The impact of different religious cultures, Catholicism in particular, as well as the more rapid spread of Marxist ideas affected the growth and thoughts of feminism in important ways. The strength of the class system in Britain was also an important factor in determining the particular course of individuals' lives. European feminism thus developed in different areas and at a different pace than in England.

In England, the stage had been set as early as the 1850s when the first trickle of organized feminism began lapping against the floodgates. By the turn of the century, those women and their successors had achieved important gains and created a new political movement which understood that sexual difference had been used to sustain weakness but could equally be harnessed to exploit strength.

What a magnificent roll-call of names rings down from the fifties and sixties! Names of pioneer women who set valiantly to work to clear the ground of the weeds and rubbish of centuries and with infinite perseverance to beat out a path to a juster and fuller existence for their sex.[11]

Feminism in nineteenth-century England served a number of important ends for women generally. It articulated within an organized form the crucial changes without which women could achieve neither political justice nor personal freedom. It maintained that the domestic ideology which had severed those two ideals conceptually and on the basis of gender was morally bankrupt. It met the needs of women, single and married and of all shades of political opinion, to find common ground and through that the strength to hit back at a long tradition of subjugation. Above all, it served as a model of alternative political and personal behaviour which valued a pragmatic humanitarianism, whatever its limitations, over the politics of domination.

Notes and references

1 Ethel Snowden, *The Feminist Movement* (1911), p. 69.
2 Marion Holmes, *Lydia Becker. A Cameo Life Sketch* (Women's Freedom League, 1913), p. 1.
3 H. M. Swanwick, *The Future of the Women's Movement* (2nd edition, London, 1914), pp. 2–3.
4 See Sheila Jeffreys, *The Spinster and Her Enemies. Feminism and Sexuality 1880–1930* (London, 1985); and Lucy Bland, 'Marriage Laid Bare: Middle-Class Women and Marital Sex 1880s–1914,' in Jane Lewis (ed.), *Labour and Love. Women's Experience of*

Home and Family, 1850–1940 (Oxford, 1986), pp. 123–46 for a detailed study of the organizations and activities of this period.

5 Martha Vicinus, *Independent Women. Work and Community for Single Women 1850–1920* (London, 1985), Chapter 7.

6 Snowden, *The Feminist Movement*, p. 21.

7 Constance L. Maynard, *We Women. A Golden Hope* (London, n.d., ?1924), p. 131.

8 Swanwick, *The Future of the Women's Movement*, p. 5.

9 Richard M. Titmuss, 'The Position of Women: Some Vital Statistics,' in M. Flinn and T. C. Smout (eds), *Essays in Social History* (Oxford, 1974), pp. 277–89 (p. 279).

10 British Library, Additional Manuscript 47451, f. 35, Elizabeth Wolstenholme Elmy to Harriet McIlquham, 13 December 1896.

11 Holmes, *Lydia Becker*, p. 1.

Further reading

In the past ten years or so, the number of books appearing on women, whether about their general position or about their protests, has burgeoned. Most of those which deal with women's protests, however, have concentrated on specific areas rather than sought to provide general accounts of the ideas of the women's movement. Ray Strachey's *The Cause. A Short History of the Women's Movement in Great Britain* was published in 1928 (a 1978 reprint is now available) and remained the only general textbook on the subject for many years. In the 1960s, a few useful though pedestrian accounts appeared. Josephine Kamm's *Rapiers and Battleaxes. The Women's Movement and Its Aftermath* (London, 1966) is perhaps the most thorough. See also *The Petticoat Rebellion. A Century of Struggle for Women's Rights* (London, 1967) by Marian Ramelson. More recently, the work of Richard Evans (*The Feminists. Women's Emancipation Movements in Europe, America and Australasia 1840–1920*, Kent, 1979) and Olive Banks (*Faces of Feminism. A Study of Feminism as a Social Movement*, Oxford, 1981) have shifted work from the merely narrative to a fuller discussion of the political perspectives of feminism, an exercise which J. A. and Olive Banks had begun in their article 'Feminism and Social Change – A Case Study of a Social Movement,' in G. K. Zollschan and W. Hirsch (eds), *Explorations in Social Change* (London, 1964), pp. 547–69. Jane Rendall's sensitive analysis of an earlier period of feminist thought provides an invaluable setting for the period, in her *The Origins of Modern Feminism: Women in Britain, France and the United States, 1780–1860* (Hampshire, 1985). Looking forward, David Rubinstein's *Before the Suffragettes. Women's Emancipation in the 1890s* (Brighton, 1986) is a thorough and exhaustive study which will help us follow through events and personalities from the Victorian to the Edwardian period. Patricia Hollis's anthology *Women in Public: The Women's Movement 1850–1900* (London,

1979) is a useful collection where one can gain a sense of women's own voices in this period.

Writings on the educational movement among women have, again, experienced something of a renaissance in recent years. Josephine Kamm's *Hope Deferred. Girls' Education in English History* (London, 1965) remains a useful survey and Margaret Bryant's more recent work *The Unexpected Revolution. A Study in the History of the Education of Women and Girls in the Nineteenth Century* (London, 1979) includes a fascinating look at the emergence of a close feminist network in this area of campaigning. These general works can now be supplemented with a number of interesting additions to the literature. Joan Burstyn (*Victorian Education and the Ideal of Womanhood*, London, 1980) and Carol Dyhouse (*Girls Growing Up in Late Victorian and Edwardian England*, London, 1981) both offer a more critical analysis of the ideological role of education in creating femininity, and of the part feminist educationalists played in promoting or rejecting dominant values. Joyce S. Pedersen's 'The Reform of Women's Secondary and Higher Education: Institutional Change and Social Values in Mid and Late Victorian England,' in *History of Education Quarterly*, Spring 1979, pp. 61–91, is a fascinating contribution to the debate and deals additionally with the impact of the new schooling on the women staff. Her 'Schoolmistresses and Headmistresses: Elites and Education in Nineteenth-Century England', *Journal of British Studies*, XV (1975) 1, pp. 135–62, evaluates the new powers which professional attitudes accorded to women teachers in this period.

The political scene, represented by women's incursion into local government and the demand for parliamentary suffrage, has been neglected except in so far as the story serves as a prelude to the excitement of the militancy of the Edwardian era. Constance Rover's *Women's Suffrage and Party Politics in Britain* (London, 1967) and David Morgan's *Suffragists and Liberals. The Politics of Women's Suffrage in Britain* (Oxford, 1975) both deal with the parliamentary end of the issue, as does Brian Harrison's more recent 'Women's Suffrage at Westminster 1866–1928,' in Michael Bentley and John Stevenson (eds), *High and Low Politics in Modern Britain. Ten Studies* (Oxford, 1983), pp. 80–122. Barbara Caine's work has been important in redressing the balance, concentrating on the women's end of the campaign rather than the men's, and her 'Feminism, Suffrage and the Nineteenth-Century

English Women's Movement', *Women's Studies International Forum* **5** (1982) 6, pp. 537–50 is of particular interest.

The activity around local politics has been a sadly neglected area, and Patricia Hollis's forthcoming volume on women in local government will be a welcome new venture. Anne-Marie Turnbull's article ' "So extremely like parliament": the work of the women members of the London School Board, 1870–1904', in the London Feminist History Group's *The Sexual Dynamics of History. Men's Power, Women's Resistance* (London, 1983) gives an account of the problems elected women faced within their chosen sphere of activity. Little else on this subject, alas, is available.

Women's work remains a relatively ill-documented field but there have been some forays into this daunting area. Ivy Pinchbeck's *Women Workers and the Industrial Revolution, 1750–1850* (London, 1930, and reprinted 1981) remains a helpful general text with Lee Holcombe's *Victorian Ladies at Work. Middle-Class Working Women in England and Wales, 1850–1914* (Newton Abbot, 1973) balancing the picture with an account of the non-manual sector. More recently, Angela John's *Unequal Opportunities. Women's Employment in England 1800–1918* (Oxford, 1986) has a varied and interesting selection of essays held together very effectively by her fine introduction. There are few books on feminist campaigns in this area; only the attempts made by women to gain access to the medical profession and women's unionization have been covered in any depth. The volumes which deal with the medical women are largely descriptive; E. Moberley Bell's *Storming the Citadel. The Rise of the Woman Doctor* (London, 1953) is a thorough account.

This is one area where working-class women have fared rather better, though these books are best read in conjunction as none are really adequate singly. Barbara Drake's *Women in Trade Unions*, first published in 1920 and reprinted in 1984, is a good general text, and was for many years the only voice in a veritable desert. Indeed, Sarah Boston's *Women Workers and the Trade Union Movement* (London, 1980) was prompted by her difficulties in finding information about women in existing texts on the history of the trade union movement. Norbert Soldon provides some useful general material in *Women in British Trade Unions 1874–1976* (Dublin, 1978) and though James A. Schmiechen's *Sweated Industries and Sweated Labour. The London Clothing Trades*

1860–1914 (London, 1984) is a concentrated monograph, it none the less provides sensitive insights into the factors prohibiting female unionization in this period. Ellen Mappen's book *Helping Women At Work. The Women's Industrial Council 1889–1914* (London, 1985) offers a detailed study of a feminist body of the period and suggests a way of distinguishing distinctive feminist positions at a time when working-class women were just gaining an effective voice.

The last few years have seen a marked increase in the publication of books on various areas of the sexual and moral debate and while J. A. and Olive Banks' pioneer study *Feminism and Family Planning in Victorian England* (New York, 1964) is still interesting reading, there can be no doubt that it has been superseded. The collection of essays edited by Jane Lewis under the title *Labour and Love. Women's Experience of Home and Family 1850–1940* (Oxford, 1986) offers a good idea of current interests in the area. Judith Walkowitz's *Prostitution and Victorian Society. Women, class and the state* (Cambridge, 1980) remains by far the most exciting and provocative of the volumes now available on the Contagious Diseases Acts agitation and indeed, on the whole issue of prostitution. Sheila Jeffreys' quirky *The Spinster and Her Enemies. Feminism and Sexuality 1880–1930* (London, 1985) provides invaluable and otherwise inaccessible material on the social purity movement which grew so rapidly in the wake of the anti-CD campaigns. A cogent analysis of the intervention of the state in 'private' affairs is provided in 'Patriarchal Aspects of Nineteenth-Century State Formation: Property Relations, Marriage and Divorce and Sexuality', an article by Rachel Harrison and Frank Mort in Philip Corrigan (ed.), *Capitalism, State Formation and Marxist Theory. Historical Investigations* (London, 1980), pp. 79–109. This provides a useful crossover from the activities of the feminists to the role of the state in the policing of such areas. Mary Shanley's article on marriage and divorce (' "One Must Ride Behind": Married Women's Rights and the Divorce Act of 1857', *Victorian Studies*, **XXV** (1982) 3, pp. 355–76) explains the early controversy over dissolving the ties of marriage and its implications for women and for the family, and Iris Minor, in her article 'Working-Class Women and Matrimonial Law Reform, 1890–1914,' (in D. E. Martin and D. Rubinstein (eds), *Ideology and the Labour Movement. Essays Presented to*

John Saville (London, 1979, pp. 103–24) reminds us of the operation of the class system even in these areas.

In this, as in all those aspects of feminist struggle where government played a role, a study of the relevant parliamentary papers will repay itself handsomely. The Royal Commissions reporting on and investigating education, employment, prostitution and the like not only betray over and over again the thinking which feminists set out to counter in their campaigns, but on occasion also admit the feminist voice. The evidence of Josephine Butler before the Royal Commission on the Operation of the Contagious Diseases Acts, or Emily Davies before the Commission on Secondary Education, makes vividly dramatic reading and brings to life the debates most effectively. New material in this area is constantly appearing, and not before time. Much of it is experimental in form or in method; whatever its position, if it too can breathe life into the history of feminism it can only enrich our understanding.

Index